D1325758

# WRITERS AND CRITICS

*Chief Editor*

A. NORMAN JEFFARES

*Advisory Editors*

DAVID DAICHES

C. P. SNOW

THOMAS HARDY wrote fourteen novels, about forty short stories and nearly a thousand poems: and since the publication of the earliest of them they have been the centre of controversy. In a lively book, Mr Wing claims that despite Hardy's reticence his novels and poems are still as exciting today as when he shocked the prim with *Tess of the d'Urbevilles* and *Jude the Obscure.*

George Wing, a graduate of the University of Durham, has since service in the infantry in the Second World War, taught English in Persia, Ghana and Kenya. He is now Head of the Department of English at the Royal College, Nairobi.

# HARDY

GEORGE WING

OLIVER AND BOYD
EDINBURGH AND LONDON

OLIVER AND BOYD LTD
Tweeddale Court
Edinburgh 1

39A Welbeck Street
London W. 1


First published 1963

Printed in Great Britain for Oliver and Boyd Ltd
by Robert MacLehose and Co. Ltd, Glasgow

# CONTENTS

## ACKNOWLEDGMENTS

For permission to quote from Hardy's works acknowledgment is due to Macmillan & Co. Ltd.

The photograph on the front cover is reproduced by permission of Radio Times Hulton Picture Library.

G.W.

## ABBREVIATED TITLES
## BY WHICH HARDY'S WORKS
### ARE CITED IN THE TEXT

| | | |
|---|---|---|
| C.M. | = | *A Changed Man, The Waiting Supper, and Other Tales.* |
| C.P. | = | *Collected Poems.* |
| D. | = | *The Dynasts.* |
| D.R. | = | *Desperate Remedies.* |
| F.M.C. | = | *Far from the Madding Crowd.* |
| G.N.D. | = | *A Group of Noble Dames.* |
| H.E. | = | *The Hand of Ethelberta.* |
| J.O. | = | *Jude the Obscure.* |
| L. | = | *A Laodicean.* |
| L.L.I. | = | *Life's Little Ironies.* |
| M.C. | = | *The Mayor of Casterbridge.* |
| P.B.E. | = | *A Pair of Blue Eyes.* |
| R.N. | = | *The Return of the Native.* |
| T.D. | = | *Tess of the d'Urbervilles.* |
| T.M. | = | *The Trumpet-Major.* |
| T.T. | = | *Two on a Tower.* |
| U.G.T. | = | *Under the Greenwood Tree.* |
| W. | = | *The Woodlanders.* |
| W.B. | = | *The Well-Beloved.* |
| W.T. | = | *Wessex Tales.* |

### OTHER ABBREVIATED TITLES

| | | |
|---|---|---|
| A.J.G. | = | A. J. Guerard, *Thomas Hardy: The Novels and Stories.* |
| F.E.H.(I). | = | Florence Emily Hardy, *The Early Life of Thomas Hardy, 1840–91.* |
| F.E.H.(II). | = | Florence Emily Hardy, *The Later Years of Thomas Hardy, 1892–1928.* |

# CHAPTER I

# THE VILLAGE ATHEIST

There are aspects of Hardy's life which he did his best to shield from public scrutiny; and the very fact that, in most of his novels and stories, and in many of his poems, he weights sexual encounter with bitterness and a sense of predestined failure, entices us to explore those shadows in his own life which might throw paradoxical light on to his somewhat morbid acceptance of marital foredoom. This is not for one moment intended to over-estimate the importance of personal accident or experience: too much emphasis can be, and has been, given to such things: there are so many unseens about the conditioning of human personality, and hence human attitudes, that a small illumination on a contributory influencing is all that is hoped for. For this purpose Hardy's boyhood, his architectural apprenticeship both in the West country and in London, and his early to middle married life, may hold keys; but before examining what appear to be the most significant concealments and repressions, a rapid, but necessarily restricted and selective survey of his largely unadventurous life, may be of value.

Hardy was born at Higher Bockhampton in the parish of Stinsford in Dorset or, as it is called in Hardy's fictive geography, *South Wessex*. Dorchester or *Casterbridge* was not many miles away. A certain constitutional weakness persisted in boyhood; and because Hardy was so frail, he did not go to school until the age of eight. He attended first Bockhampton School, erected by the "lady of the manor." She was Julia Augusta Martin, and there developed between Hardy and her a peculiar attachment which was sustained for many years. After a year at "her school," however, he moved to a Dorchester day school to which he used to walk, like Jude, daily along the country lanes. Lord David Cecil attributes great importance to these early conditions; they constituted, as it were, a literary placenta:

> For the plots of Hardy's books are as much conditioned by his upbringing as are his setting and characters. His comedy turns on the genial, farcical humours of village life. His tragedy is village tragedy. . . .[1]

Apart from the bigness of comedy and tragedy, there are the peasant accessories: there is witchcraft: there are midsummer rites: "while country customs and ceremonies and gaieties, carol-singing, harvest homes, maypoles and mummers' plays, are scattered broadcast over his pages."[1] A close intimacy with the country and its ways and traditions lasted for the first twenty-two years of his life. At sixteen, "though he had just begun to be interested in French and the Latin classics,"[2] he left school and went into the office of John Hicks, a Dorchester architect, but still lived at home and walked to and from work. It was during these early morning walks, in summer especially when he rose at four, that Hardy, with extraordinary self-discipline, developed his classical education from its fitful school beginnings. All his spare time, which poached into his sleeping time, was devoted to an acquisition of learning. His Spartan dedication, his rustic doggedness compare with the long hard hours spent by the peasants in the field, but it is also biographical evidence of a force which Hardy was to use later with great effect in his novels. This new thrust, which he often showed in a malevolent light, was the intrusion of education and sophistication into a peasant land of ancient simplicity and traditional wisdom. It upset the old patterns. It turned Grace Melbury against her old sweetheart Giles Winterbourne. It made Tess ashamed of her mother and father. It drove Jude to beat his head against unsympathetic Oxford walls. Yet in retrospect Hardy seems justifiably proud of his own assimilation of book learning, although it could, by its revelation of the absurdity of closely guarded social barriers, provoke resentment in him, and near-tragic outcomes in his writings.

Two other people who must be mentioned briefly in this first country phase of Hardy's life, are the Rev. William Barnes, the Dorset poet and philologist who "kept school" next to Hicks' office, and Horace Moule, "of Queen's College, Cambridge, just then beginning practice as an author and reviewer." From Barnes, friendly, pedagogic, informed, Hardy might have caught something of the infection of poetry and of the use of dialect as a literary device: it was at any rate a literary connexion and his first. Moule had a deeper but darker influence which persisted long after his death in 1875 (he committed suicide in his rooms at Queen's shortly after Hardy had visited him there). He was the son of the Vicar of Fordington, a village now swallowed up by Dorchester. His sophistication, his learning, his serious but kindly criticism meant much to Hardy. But so too did his fits of acute melancholia: he was in the van of an age of neuroses and Hardy was exceptionally affected by his sporadic descents to lonely despair. Perhaps some of the side-effects of this friendship cause the darkening of some of the novels.

Hardy then was not quite unlicked and raw when he went to London in 1862, but he was essentially a country lad. Not a bumpkin, not Hodge, but one who had experienced the plainness of country life as well as appreciated its delights: one who had schooled himself rigorously along traditional classical lines: one who had been brought up in Church of England orthodoxy, but who was now reading or about to read Darwin, Mill, Huxley. He went to a London architect, Mr Arthur Blomfield "with whom Hardy was to keep up a friendship for near on forty years,"[3] but this particular phase of association—working in Blomfield's office—lasted only until 1867. During this time he progressed well with his architecture; he wrote an essay "How I Built Myself a House," which was published in *Chambers's Journal* in 1865; he composed some early poems, some of which (among them "Hap," "In Vision I Roamed," "Neutral Tones," "Her Reproach") have survived; he studied French for a few terms under Professor Stievenard at King's College; he went to Radical meetings, to theatres and art galleries: but by and large he was not basically happy during this phase of his life. It is, however, a period in which the record has significant hints as well as significant blanks. Certainly his health deteriorated. Dedicated reading evening after evening at Westbourne Park Villas took its toll: "When he visited his friends in Dorset they were shocked at the pallor which sheeted a countenance formerly ruddy with health."[4] In July 1867 he went back to Hicks in Dorchester. It was not, however, in the capacity of full architectural employment, for, temporarily discarding poetry, he had now turned to prose fiction, and he worked only intermittently at Hicks' office. He had come to one of those cross-roads of decision in life and what he needed was "a clear call to him which course in life to take—the course he loved, and which was his natural instinct, that of letters, or the course all practical wisdom dictated, that of architecture."[5]

His first attempt at a novel—*The Poor Man and the Lady* —brought rejection from the publisher and criticism from Meredith, but also sufficient encouragement to avoid the complete dampening of nascent fires: his last work as an architect—a church restoration job in Cornwall—brought him a wife. Vital decisions in more than one respect had been taken.

1868 to 1896, *The Poor Man and the Lady* to *Jude the Obscure*, are years of intense literary activity: all the novels and most of the stories were written in this period. After reading the youthful satire, *The Poor Man and the Lady*, Meredith advised its young author "not to 'nail his colours to the mast' so definitely in a first book"[6] and suggested that he should write another novel altogether. Evelyn Hardy, among others, has done some admirable reconstruction on the fate of this early work:

> Weary of the vicissitudes of *The Poor Man*, Hardy decided to do the latter (write another novel). The result was *Desperate Remedies*. But he did not destroy *The Poor Man and the Lady*, whose latter history is as complicated as its earlier. He dismembered it, used portions of it in three ensuing novels, and published an emasculated form of it as *An Indiscretion in the Life of an Heiress* ten years later.[7]

For good or ill Meredith's advice was taken and Hardy moved from social satire, which attacked on all fronts, to an incident-thick "sensational" novel after the manner of Wilkie Collins and with financial backing from the author (an act of courage this) *Desperate Remedies* was published anonymously by the hard-headed Tinsley, in 1871.

Meantime romance had set in. Hardy strongly denies that there is much biographical connexion between his own experience and the setting and characters of *A Pair of Blue Eyes*, but there are nevertheless remarkable parallels in person, incident and situation. On Hicks' death, G. R. Crickmay had taken over the firm and from time to time Hardy assisted him. Crickmay invited him to take on some work at St Juliot in Cornwall and Hardy almost refused because at this point he had just about given up architecture and was immersed, at his mother's old house, in the manuscript of *Desperate Remedies*. The final persuasion to go is almost of Hardyan fictive contrivance for, at St Juliot, he met Emma Lavinia Gifford, sister-in-law of the Rev. Caddell Holder, the Rector of St Juliot.

The acquaintanceship soon moved into a friendship which ripened quickly. There is an interesting account by Emma of this courtship reproduced in *The Early Life*[8] but since she did not write it until 1911 (just before her death) it must be remembered that ancient events are seen through the nostalgic eyes of an old lady. Back in 1870 however, Emma was thrilled with her architect who was also a poet and a novelist, and she helped in copying out manuscripts. They did not marry until 1874.

The basic artist was now rough-cast, and although there was obviously to be development and maturation in his writing, the clay of the original Hardy had been fired: the stamp is on *Desperate Remedies* as patently as it is on *Jude the Obscure*. There were twenty years or so of composition of prose fiction (with poetry not entirely neglected): new titles of magazine serials (the original form of most of the novels—because they were a paying proposition) appeared regularly: criticism varied from the harsh to the enthusiastic but Hardy's popularity grew steadily, and his financial position was removed from the edge of precariousness.

In 1872 *Under the Greenwood Tree* was published, again anonymously, again by Tinsley, and was reasonably well reviewed. This was the first of the essentially pastoral writings; it was originally entitled *The Mellstock Quire*, and, with its fictive parallels and echoes of rustic dance and ecclesiastical music, it is closely and nostalgically associated with Bockhampton and Stinsford. The serialisation of *A Pair of Blue Eyes* followed in *Tinsley's Magazine* with the promise of a three-volume novel publication in 1873. About this time Hardy met Leslie Stephen, "the editor of the *Cornhill*—by that time well known as a man of letters, *Saturday* reviewer, and Alpine climber."[9] Over the years Stephen's counsel impressed Hardy, who took note of it: but Stephen's personal tragedies also affected the author's sensitive nature almost as darkly as Moule's had done. Stephen asked for a serial for the *Cornhill* and this was the beginning of *Far from the Madding Crowd*, which was published in November 1874 and was well received. Hardy and Emma had married a month previously and after a honeymoon in France had returned to live in Surbiton. With the responsibility of a wife, he had "to live by the pen" and had "to consider popularity." He rushed, therefore, into a new venture completely different from anything he had written so far. Hardy did not wish for ever to be associated with sheep and shepherds: he knew London well, had travelled on the continent and had moved in passably smart society. The desire for popularity, though not for ambition's sake, and the search for another theme and situation, led to the appearance of *The Hand of Ethelberta—A Comedy in Chapters*. In the same year, 1876, he bought "a pretty cottage overlooking the Dorset Stour—called 'Riverside Villa' "[10] at Sturminster Newton. Here Hardy and Emma spent their "happiest time" until March of 1878: certain poems from *Moments of Vision* were composed and *The Return of the Native* written and serialised in a monthly magazine *Belgravia*. They went back to live in London, and Hardy looked at some of the Napoleonic material that he had been getting together (it was ultimately intended for *The Dynasts*) and used it skeletally for *The Trumpet-Major*. In the same year as this publication, he fell ill from an internal haemorrhage, but since he had begun and committed himself to *A Laodicean* for *Harper's Magazine*, he continued to dictate, despite pain and sickness, succeeding chapters to Emma who "worked bravely both at writing and nursing."[11] *Two on a Tower* was printed serially in the *Atlantic Monthly* in 1882, and in the following year Hardy began to build himself a house, Max Gate, near Dorchester. He was homing now on the county town of his birthplace, and almost inevitably *The Mayor of Casterbridge* followed, first in the *Graphic* and then in two volumes in 1886: "Here, like old Mr. Barnes, he considered gods and men from Dorchester as the centre, with the Hardyan difference that, for literary purposes, Dorchester was still a Roman as well as an English capital."[12] The high creative pressure did not slacken and in the following year *The Woodlanders* appeared. At this point, Hardy, as a novelist, paused for breath, but apart from novels he had been writing poems and stories; and in 1888 the first collected edition of the stories, *Wessex Tales*, appeared. The *Tales* included "The Distracted Preacher," "Fellow Townsmen," "The Three Strangers," and "The Withered Arm." Stories like "The Romantic Adventures of a Milkmaid," which were to appear in later collections, had also been published in magazines. It had been a period of immense output, massive and ranging far, and from an entry in his notebook on 31 Dec. 1887 we gather that Hardy had achieved confidence in himself as a writer of fiction, "whatever that may be worth."[13] This self-depreciation of his novels was consistently maintained.

Despite a certain confidence, and despite the appraisal of enthusiastic critics like Havelock Ellis and Lionel Johnson, Hardy was still sensitive to what he considered unjust reviewing. Even as late as 1922 he writes of "impotent or mischievous criticism" as:

> . . . the satirizing of individuality, the lack of whole-seeing in contemporary estimates of poetry and kindred work, the knowingness affected by junior reviewers, the overgrowth of meticulousness in their peerings for an opinion, as if it were a cultivated habit in them to scrutinize the tool-marks and be blind to the building. . . .[14]

The reactionary storms, although there was also certain acclamation, generated by the appearance of *Tess of the d'Urbervilles* and *Jude the Obscure* published in unbowdlerised book form in 1891 and 1896 respectively, caused him to abandon novel writing altogether. Before drawing a line under the prose account, we must notice in 1891 the second collection of stories, *A Group of Noble Dames*, where Hardy ventures into country houses, not always with social ease, but mostly retaining the old magic of a teller of tales. Three years later there was a further collection, *Life's Little Ironies*, with its delightful "A Few Crusted Characters" and with an ingenious version of an old sexual theme in "On the Western Circuit." The final novel, *The Well-Beloved*, an amusing exercise in time and plot, had been mainly composed earlier and was published in 1897.

Reasonably financially secure, Hardy turned to the calmer atmosphere of poetry, short stories, and the modest acceptance of accumulating honours. *Wessex Poems*, which contained some of his earliest poetry, was published in 1898 and was reviewed "mostly in a friendly tone."[15] In 1901 *Poems of the Past and Present* appeared. The Boer War did not seem to have quite the same depressive impact on Hardy that the Great War did, but, as such poems as "Drummer Hodge"[16] reveal, he could suffer vicariously with the other ranks, especially with Wessex soldiers. The climax of his formal philosophising in poetry is reached with his submission of *The Dynasts: A Drama of the Napoleonic Wars* in three parts which appeared in 1903–4, 1906 and 1908. *Time's Laughing-Stocks and other Verses* (1909), as the satirical title indicates, contained some bitter ballad-like anecdotes of sexual infidelity and of the wayward instability of marriage. Whatever the tensions or distresses in Hardy's own marriage, they were not to last much longer. Emma died in November 1912. Illuminatingly Hardy's grief was deep and genuine as his bewilderment was great. In the *Poems of 1912–13* with the sub-title, *Veteris vestigia flammae* which were included in the volume *Satires of Circumstance, Lyrics and Reveries* (1914) there are some elegiac love poems of a high order, unforced and plaintively sincere with just an isolated hint to indicate that some of the fault may have been his:

B

Well, well! *All's past amend,*
Unchangeable. It must go.
I seem but a dead man held on end
To sink down soon. . . . O you could not know
That such swift fleeing
No soul foreseeing—
Not even I—would undo me so![17]

Hardy was now seventy-two, and his life and household
degenerated into mourning, disorganisation, and point-
lessness: two years later, however, he married Florence
Emily Dugdale, and order was restored with astonishing
swiftness to his domestic affairs.

Meantime he had got together another collection of
stories (all of which had been previously separately published) under the title of *A Changed Man, The Waiting
Supper and Other Tales* (1913). One of them, "The Duke's
Reappearance," is based on an allegedly true story concerning the Duke of Monmouth and the Swetman family
(Hardy's ancestors on his mother's side). The Great War,
of course, broke out, but the poetic inspiration of a man
in his seventies remained unchecked. *Moments of Vision
and Miscellaneous Verses* appeared in 1917. One of them,
"Men who March Away," written in 1914, and having
caught something of the jingoism that was in the air, was
first published in *The Times* and became enormously
popular. But this attitude was largely superficial. Had he
been able to forecast the outbreak of war, "he would
probably not have ended *The Dynasts* as he did end it,"
because war had "destroyed all Hardy's belief in the
gradual ennoblement of man" and had given "the *coup
de grace* to any conception he may have nourished of a
fundamental ultimate Wisdom at the back of things."[18]
Yet a few years later he was contradicting such statements,
in part at least, in the *Apology* to *Late Lyrics and Earlier*
which appeared in 1922.

Honours were bestowed. Oxford and Cambridge conferred degrees and honorary fellowships and the spirit of Jude was to some extent appeased. The King awarded him the Order of Merit on his seventieth birthday. On his seventy-eighth a large number of living poets presented to him a volume of poetic tributes. The Balliol Players came annually to Max Gate and played Greek tragedy on the lawns. The extraordinarily immense energy was not quite burnt up. Although the second Mrs Hardy entitles his last decade *Life's Decline*, there was a prolonged and ever flickering coda. Three more volumes of verse: *The Queen of Cornwall* (a verse drama) in 1923; *Human Shows* in 1925; and finally *Winter Words* in 1928.

There is a moving account of the last days of his life by Florence Emily: and this must have been truly her work. The great man was at last beyond dictation or revision.

I have tried to indicate the more obvious influences which find themselves permeated in Hardy's writings. Church music echoes about the pages: passages spring to unsophisticated gaiety in rural song and dance: the countryside and its customs and a minute observation of them: London (surprisingly—because Hardy is popularly thought of as a teller of pastoral tales): architecture— especially churches and church restoration: the Bible: the nineteenth-century philosophers and scientists, who induced an uneasy, monistic thinking, a determinism, an unacceptance of an overall Benevolent Controller. These are indeed obvious and are fully recorded by Hardy and others. But there are omissions from the register. We are confronted with sombre question-marks.

In his novels and stories, and in many poems, Hardy was chiefly concerned with sexual mischance, sometimes overlaid with romantic pastoral love but nearly always diseased with gloomy prognosis. There may or may not be a hidden psychological reason for this attitude. Most written evidence of this sort of self-revelation has been destroyed but occasionally an informative piece escapes:

*June 2.* My 25th birthday. Not very cheerful. Feel as if I have lived a long time and done very little. Walked about by moonlight in the evening. Wondered what woman, if any, I should be thinking about in five years' time.[19]

This entry could be completely innocent, the sort of thing that any serious, introspective, lonely young man might set down in his diary: but about this passage Edmund Blunden writes:

That signifies that in much less time there would have been a woman in the case, or that there had been one recently; but the records are silent, except the few poems which have escaped destruction, and they reflect the obvious. Hardy, disciplined to a fault, cautious perhaps to a fault, in spite of his excellence and outward charm, was in love with someone who preferred other approaches and, in those days it may be, another social prospect. This is not mere biographical probing. The writings of Thomas Hardy, the proportion of sun or gloom in them, depended much upon his felicity or frustration in finding a mate: it was an inherited, it was an individual crisis. But he did not talk of this in Blomfield's office.[20]

Blunden makes certain conjecture and from his starting-point I should like to extend the area of possibility. It would seem that this time in London was the most likely for any possible sexual adventure although there could have been an Arabella-Judish episode before he came up. The "lady of the manor" idolatry can be discounted in this context. Hardy is far too open about it and it was a very understandable attachment. The permutations of sexual probabilities and of unlikely promiscuities in London are formidable. Had one or more "respectable" love affairs gone wrong? Had he ever, like Angel Clare, "plunged into eight-and-forty hours' dissipation with a stranger"? And then been inordinately revolted both by the stranger and by himself? Was he a furiously sensitive man scorned? Had he got into an entanglement with a married woman? Had he met a teasing epicene like Sue Bridehead who had lived with a Christminster graduate but had kept him sexually at bay? Or was there some psychological or physical deficiency which tethered him when he would have galloped forward? All are possibilities: all could be ruled out. The sexual bitterness nevertheless stains his writing.

There are two earlier scraps of information which are probably insignificant but, because of the shortage of clues, might be seized upon by a psychological investigator. Hardy was at times almost anti-social:

He loved being alone, but often, to his concealed discomfort, some of the other boys would volunteer to accompany him on his homeward journey to Bockhampton. How much this irked him he recalled long years after.[21]

His sensitiveness extended to a horror of physical contact:

He tried also to avoid being touched by his playmates. One lad, with more insight than the rest, discovered the fact: "Hardy, how is it that you do not like us to touch you?" This peculiarity never left him, and to the end of his life he disliked even the most friendly hand being laid on his arm or his shoulder.[21]

Finally there is his own marriage which to begin with was of the stuff of romance and idyllic passion. His early writings could not have been influenced by this union except optimistically and benevolently. Later we know that life was not always happy with Emma, and in 1877 there is one recorded plaint, the reason for which is locked forever in the privacy of two people:

*August 13.* We hear that Jane, our late servant, is soon to have a baby. Yet never a sign of one is there for us.[22]

And up to Emma's death in 1912 there never was. Hardy was preoccupied with ancestry: this lack of an heir could have been more than normally saddening but there could heve been even sadder contiguities. We know too that Emma was an unwarranted snob and considered that she had married beneath her: that she was all for the gay life, while her prospering and famous husband demanded no lionising but required only the seclusion and quiet of the countryside: that she almost certainly had phases of near-insanity. But there is no easy interpretation of these factors. Irritated and depressed as Hardy must have been from time to time, there is no gainsaying his genuine grief expressed at her death in *Veteris vestigia flammae*.

When all is said and done, and even after the most myopic peering into the shadows, A. J. Guerard may well be right:

> Thus the facts of Hardy's life are very nearly as irrelevant to an understanding of his novels as the literary tendencies of the age; we look largely in vain for a figure in the carpet of fact.[23]

He further claims: "It would be dangerous to put much personal emphasis on Hardy's concern with sexual betrayal, infidelity, and concealment." But he has a later qualification:

> Even when we have made these reservations, however, Hardy's census of betrayal remains exceptionally full and detailed. There is little to be learned from an enumeration of true lovers thrown over or of illegitimate children and hasty marriages concealed. The most interesting clue (if it is a clue) lies in the shifting role of the woman from that of the fickle betrayed to that of the simple-hearted betrayed, from Fancy Day and Elfride Swancourt to Marty South and Tess.[24]

It is needless to state the critical eminence of Blunden, Cecil, and Guerard: yet on this issue they are at opposite poles. The question probably cannot be resolved; but to conclude this commentary on Hardy's life and as a pointer to an examination of his writings, I emphasise and extend Guerard's tenet: if Hardy's portraiture of women goes through a process of increasing and cumulative appreciation, then one factor remains constant: that factor is sexual betrayal, largely, but not always, the result of an incompatible marriage or unhappy alliance.

## REFERENCES

1. Lord David Cecil, *Hardy the Novelist*, 1960, pp. 17–18.
2. *F.E.H.(I)*., p. 35.
3. *F.E.H.(I)*., p. 48.
4. *F.E.H.(I)*., p. 70.
5. *F.E.H.(I)*., p. 79.
6. *F.E.H.(I)*., p. 80.
7. Evelyn Hardy, *Thomas Hardy: A Critical Biography*, 1954, p. 89.
8. *F.E.H.(I)*., pp. 88 ff. A fuller account of Emma's memoirs can be found in *Some Recollections by Emma Hardy together with Some Relevant Poems by Thomas Hardy*, ed. Evelyn Hardy and Robert Gittings, 1961.
9. *F.E.H.(I)*., p. 125.
10. *F.E.H.(I)*., p. 147.
11. *F.E.H.(I)*., p. 188.
12. Edmund Blunden, *Thomas Hardy*, 1941, p. 54.
13. *F.E.H.(I)*., p. 267.
14. *C.P.*, p. 530.
15. *F.E.H.(II)*., p. 76.
16. *C.P.*, p. 83.
17. *C.P.*, p. 319. (my italics).
18. *F.E.H.(II)*., p. 165.
19. *F.E.H.(I)*., p. 65.
20. Edmund Blunden, *op. cit.*, p. 28.
21. *F.E.H.(I)*., p. 32.
22. *F.E.H.(I)*., p. 153.
23. *A.J.G.*, p. 40.
24. *A.J.G.*, p. 42.

# CHAPTER II

# BETRAYAL AND THE
# GROTESQUE

There are over forty short stories of great diversity in length, mostly collected by Hardy into four volumes. They were written between 1874 and 1900, but they largely fall within the time-span of *The Poor Man and the Lady* and *Jude the Obscure*. Despite the not inconsiderable number of them, their importance has been, more often than not, underestimated. Of the recent critics, A. J. Guerard treats them with deference and illuminatingly, but not as a body of work—his references are broadcast: Douglas Brown devotes a section[1] to them, but sparingly refers in detail to only two stories: for the main, there is patronising or sparse allusion and this may be because Hardy himself did not apparently rate them of serious account: he certainly did not lavish on them the care and the affection, either during composition or in retrospect, with which he cosseted so many of his poems. But they have their values and, to my mind, a distinguished place in any assessment of Hardy's writings. They have a basic worth of their own, within the limits of their artistic structure, and are viable, often corrosively imaginative, pieces of fiction with a piquant evocation of place and atmosphere, and with a shrewd, if sometimes Draconian, commentary on human conduct. In them Hardy shows, perhaps more than anywhere else, a sharper perception of the ludicrous and odd in the human situation and in accident and behaviour, and yet the exceptional and abnormal are presented convincingly and with validity. Most of them are also written with a surprising economy, a quality often lacking in the greater and better-known novels. But, apart from the fact that they themselves are a justification of their own existence, they are also cardinal adjuncts to an appraisal of the novels and poems. They are both the precursors and echoes of many a theme in novel or poem. They are part of the sum of the whole creation of Hardy's writings and they are so integral, inter-related, and vital, that a consummate understanding is not possible if they are excluded from the total reckoning. If only for this, a close study of the stories is rewarding. There is revealed a surprising fictional kinship which runs through all his works. There is a remarkable association of person, incident, situation, and attitude. The meditative responses, satirical or benign, have also much in common with those of the novels. Often the essential is more crystallised and more readily apparent in the stories (and this is also true of many of the poems) because the case has to be presented more swiftly and economically.

The theme of sexual betrayal and unhappy alliances was stressed, perhaps overmuch, in the last chapter, but this human divergence from the traditionally moral is clamourously repetitive in the stories and may be as good a point as any to start from. Betrayal in a gregarious society is an imposed and unnatural act, coerced out of the betrayer by the uncontrollability of his own feelings or by hostile circumstance: the circumstance, in these stories, may be that of wedlocked incompatibility or that of the *impossibility* of ever attaining a happy alliance. In the latter case, there is often a subtler superincumbent irony in that the hoped-for happiness will inevitably go sour. Hardy protests on at least one occasion that an apparently happy marital ending will not in fact be so, but that it has been forced upon him by magazine readers, in presumably much the same way as such domestic apodoses were forced upon the fictive participants by prevailing social barbarisms. The story of "The

Distracted Preacher" is a delightfully light satire upon a Wesleyan minister: but the light handling does not conceal shabby undertones when the full implications of human betrayal are realised. Against a background of gay (which can turn violent) smuggling, Richard Stockdale, the preacher in question, falls in love with an attractive young widow, Mrs Lizzy Newbury, who is his landlady in Nether Moynton. His moral orthodoxy is severely compromised when he finds out that the liquor with which she cured his cold is contraband, and he makes a further agonising discovery that she is herself an active smuggler and goes about her illicit business dressed in her former husband's old clothes. His moral orthodoxy cannot however, withstand an overpowering sexual impulse, and in a series of comic episodes he keeps returning to her, moth-like and dog-like. Ultimately, Victorian morality wins the day and Lizzy discards her true mate, Jim Owlett, the smuggler-miller, for the sanctity and safety of the life of a parson's wife. "She studied her duties as a minister's wife with praiseworthy assiduity" and "wrote an excellent tract called *Render unto Caesar; or, The Repentant Villagers*."[2] But in 1912 Hardy added a postscript to the happy ending:

> NOTE.—The ending of this story with the marriage of Lizzy and the minister was almost *de rigeur* in an English magazine at the time of writing. But at this late date, thirty years after, it may not be amiss to give the ending that would have been preferred by the writer to the convention used above. Moreover it corresponds more closely with the true incidents of which the tale is a vague and flickering shadow. Lizzy did not, in fact, marry the minister, but—much to her credit in the author's opinion—stuck to Jim the smuggler, and emigrated with him after their marriage. . . .[2]

A woman with Lizzy's sense of fun and adventure would, despite her tracts, have been inordinately bored as the

leading moral lady in a nonconformist parish: perhaps
her incarceration into respectability, besides being a sop
to the magazine-readers, marks the beginning of latter-
day suburban neurotics.

Hindrances to a marriage sometimes take the form
of class-consciousness. Trumpery parochial snobbery
angered Hardy, but in "The Waiting Supper" (1888)
(which was written about the same time as *The Woodlanders* and contains a similar type of class conflict) he
handles the theme with restraint—even with light-hearted
mockery. Nicholas Long, an honest-John farmer, woos a
Squire's daughter, Christine Everard. Caste prejudices
prevail, and she marries Mr Bellston who socially is more
acceptable to her father. Her father dies, and her husband
deserts her in comparative poverty. Fifteen years later,
Long returns with a fortune, but his plans to marry
Christine break down because of the reported reappearance of her first husband: seventeen years after this the
skeleton of her first husband is found in a waterfall, but
still they do not marry. Christine, to spite herself, almost,
will not atone for her first betrayal, and two lost lives
slide ineffectually into decline and wastefulness. The
conclusion is at once pathetic and abject. "But occasionally he ventured to urge her to reconsider the case, though
he spoke not with the fervour of his earlier years."[3]

The twist is crueller in "On the Western Circuit"
(1891), because the betrayal does not lie essentially in the
seduction of a simple country girl in Salisbury by an up-
and-coming young man of law, but in the wilful destruction of three happinesses by an obstinate adherence to an
imposed code of conduct. It is true that Charles Bradford
Raye, the barrister, seduces Anna, a servant-girl, but his
act of human betrayal lies, perversely, in his marrying
her. Anna admits after her marriage that she is illiterate
and that her mistress wrote her love-letters for her:

The simple girl, upheld by the sense that she was indeed

married, showed her delight at finding that he was as kind as ever after the disclosure. She did not know that before his eyes he beheld as it were a galley, in which he, the fastidious urban, was chained to work for the remainder of his life, with her, the unlettered peasant, chained to his side.[4]

In some stories, apparently, Hardy takes an almost savage delight in presenting entanglements of betrothal. Our sympathy and derision become similarly entangled and we view with laughing apprehension certain humanly distorted situations. Some such occur in "Interlopers at the Knap" (1884) and "Enter a Dragoon" (1900). It is noteworthy that the latter was written when Hardy was sixty, so that his perverse enjoyment (and there seems to be no doubt about a certain mischievous enjoyment) was apparently persistently sustained. The judgment of Farmer Darton in the "Interlopers" is clouded by his sensitiveness to social prestige. Twice he betrays Sally Hall, with the consequence of wasted and lonely lives. In "Enter a Dragoon," Selina Paddock throws away any prospect of happiness by returning to the father of her illegitimate child, Serjeant-Major John Clark—"She picked up wi 'en against her father's wish, as we know, and before he got his stripes."[5] The ultimate irony is double-crowned. Selina, on a visit to Clark's grave, which she had been tending, meets unexpectedly the dragoon's legitimate widow. She, too, has been at work on the grave, and remarks witheringly: "I am sorry I pulled up your ivy-roots; but that common sort of ivy is considered a weed in my part of the country."[6] There is human paltriness here and an inverted pride in marital legitimacy: the unhappily trusting Selina is herself a helpless weed, at the mercy of the foresightless currents of sexual misadventure and faithlessness. Sometimes, however, the betrayal is not, as it were, fully consummated, and the languishing survivor compels admiration. In "A Changed

Man" (1900) Laura, a gay young thing from Casterbridge, is captivated by Captain Maumbry, a dashing
officer of the Hussars, and at first they abandon themselves to the social whirl. He, however, suddenly and
unexpectedly becomes aware of the more sober realities of
life, resigns his commission, and reads for the ministry. To
Laura's bitter disappointment, he becomes a parson and
plunges into good works, while she seeks an outlet for her
sexual energy and her desire for the gay life through an
affair with Lieutenant Vannicock. As she is about to leave
her husband, a plague hits the town, and as Maumbry
toils among the stricken, he catches the infection and dies.
Laura's act of desertion is suspended and is never
quickened again: "the insistent shadow of that unconscious one"[7] came between them and she lived and died a
widow. Sometimes, too, the expected, foredoomed, dull
ending has a quaint compassion about it and a strange
compensation which may, one must admit, be sentimental
fodder for the magazine-readers. Baptista Trewthen, the
central figure of "A Mere Interlude" (1885), a young
schoolteacher, is engaged to a rich man, much older, in
her Channel Island home. She experiences, on the main-
land, a whirlwind romance with Charles Stow which ends
with a hasty marriage. Stow is drowned almost immediately, and Baptista returns to marry Heddegan, the dull
rich merchant. The past threatens, and she confesses.
Heddegan is relieved, and, trading secrets, admits that
he has four strapping daughters by a former marriage. It
is arranged that the girls shall return to their father, and
Baptista is full of gloom: the girls turn out to be plain and
inarticulate, and she views the tutoring of them with
dismay: "In the long vista of future years she saw nothing
but dreary drudgery at her detested old trade without
prospect of reward."[8] Perhaps the story should have
ended on such a typical note of the probably unhappy,
but on this occasion Hardy is on better terms with
humanity. Baptista struggled on until there happened

"a serener season for the chastened spirit of Baptista Heddegan," and "she grew to like the girls of unpromising exterior, and from liking she got to love them."[8]

In most cases, however, the result of the betrayal is, at its best, weary years of boredom and, at its worst, excruciating distress or death. A girl's faithlessness puts Corporal Matthaus Tina of His Majesty's Regiment of York Hussars before a firing squad;[9] Dorothy, the illegitimate daughter of Sir Ashley Mottisfont, is shuttled from mother to foster-mother, then handed over to a cottage woman, and eventually marries a "respectable road-contractor";[10] Lady Caroline marries the parish-clerk's son, and after years of subterfuge and concealment loses her own son to a village girl.[11] The plots are thick with incident: some of the situations at first sight are highly improbable: but by and large the stories succeed through their very integrity, and we must resignedly accept the convincingness of this succession of faithless acts.

Another group of stories, which may or may not also contain the faithless-betrayal theme, is that which has as a common factor an element of the unusual which stretches to the incredible; what A. J. Guerard calls "anti-realism." A device which Hardy uses, not only as a peg for a fascinating story, but also as a means of stripping down pretensions, is to present the normal person in an abnormal situation: sometimes the situation is weirdly horrific, sometimes it violates probability, sometimes it crosses the irrational border and strays into the supernatural or demonic. Such stories are invariably entrancing, and their very grotesqueness intensifies, for the modern reader, their ultimate reality. Under such preternatural stresses the human character is shown more starkly, and perhaps with shrewder perception and with deeper meaning.

An outstanding story in this group is, with its mixture of tenderness and horror, "The Withered Arm" (1888). Not only are there present unhealthy and inimical forces not normally recognised or experienced within the accepted human range, but also Hardy so contrives his plot and arranges his coincidences that he is in danger of offending against all the acceptable canons of probability. A thin worn milkmaid, Rhoda Brook, has an illegitimate son by Farmer Lodge (that theme is impossible to get away from) but he does not marry her and takes to wife instead "a rosy-cheeked, tisty-tosty little body,"[12] Gertrude, a more refined girl not really cut out for the rigours of a farm. The natural human conflict lies obviously between the two women but there is an intervention in the shape of a wasting disease, supernaturally induced. As the new bride is brought triumphantly back, Rhoda in her rough cottage, tries to picture what she is like. One night she goes to bed and in a nightmare, she feels the weight of Gertrude, "with features shockingly distorted," on her chest: after a desperate struggle, she seizes the spectre by its left arm and whirls it to the floor.[13] From that moment the real Gertrude Lodge's arm begins to wither but the process took many years. Lodge's love for his young wife begins to wither too. The story is set paradoxically against the usual Wessex background with its normalcy and almost monotonous everydayness. Eventually, after taking advice from Conjuror Trendle on the "turning of blood," Gertrude, by pleas and bribery, obtains access to the body of a newly-hanged man and touches his neck. There is a surfeit of final coincidence. By chance (or in the event obviously?), Lodge and Rhoda are also present, because the corpse is that of their illegitimate son. The whole psychological impact is too much for Gertrude. "Her blood had been 'turned' indeed—too far,"[14] and she dies. The degree of improbability is admittedly high; but without demanding too great a suspension of credulity, Hardy carries the story successfully, and we are left in a state of conjecture and apprehensive speculation: in such speculation, early twentieth-century scepticism surrenders to later para-psychological possibility. But apart from abstruse considerations of this nature, Gertrude and Rhoda are, as tortured women, living characters, in whom we must believe and who wring from us compassion.

"Barbara of the House of Grebe" (1890) contains a variation on a Pygmalion theme overlaid with cruelty and horror. Edmond Willowes, the first husband of Barbara, later Lady Uplandtowers, is badly burnt and disfigured in Venice; and as she cannot even bear seeing him, he creeps away from her to die. Later, after her second marriage to Lord Uplandtowers, an Adonis-like statue of her former husband appears from Italy and she falls in love with it. When Uplandtowers discovers this, he has the image mutilated as Willowes was (" 'Neither nose nor ears, nor lips scarcely!' "),[15] and he forces her to gaze upon it night after night by candlelight until her mind and personality are beaten into submission to him. She takes, however, a queer revenge: "She bore him no less than eleven children in the nine following years, but half of them came prematurely into the world, or died a few days old; only one, a girl, attained to maturity."[16] The masculine dominance of Uplandtowers is expressed in a peevish, cruel, almost effeminate manner and with the effective use of a crude applied psychology: but Barbara's vengeful counterpoise infers a psycho-physical, prenatal malice, which is at once absurd and mordantly plausible. Mop Ollamoor's power over Car'line Aspent in "The Fiddler of the Reels" (1893) is also of a supernatural order, the vehicle of mastery being the music of Mop's fiddle. In a story whose situation moves from the middle of Stickleford village to the Great Exhibition of 1851 in London, to the Quiet Woman, a lonely roadside hostel on the lower verge of Egdon Heath, the critical point is women's, and especially Car'line's susceptibility to Mop's tunes: he manages to induce in some women, by his playing, a hysteria, an ecstasy which mounts sometimes to an epilepsy and can involve complete sexual surrender. He disappears to the mysterious realms from which he came, robbing a couple of a child and happiness.[17]

The abnormal situation sometimes involves one of the usually conventional characters in the embarrassment of acting unconventionally. There is a consequent contradiction in attitude or awkward self-debasing behaviour. Timothy Petrick suspects that his wife Annetta, "Squire Petrick's Lady" (1890), has borne an illegitimate son, and after her death in childbirth disinherits the child. Since the alleged father is of high aristocratic birth, he gradually becomes proud of this connexion and reinstates the boy. He discovers eventually that his wife suffered from delusions and is bitterly disappointed to learn that the child was his own with "the broad nostril and hollow bridge of his grandfather Timothy."[18] "The Lady Icenway" (1890) well married, rich, haughty is obliged to beg an odd favour from a sick poor Dutchman. It is true that there had been an earlier liaison between the two, but that is now buried in the past and overgrown by the splendour of Lady Icenway's position. As the years pass, she cannot produce an heir for her impotent lord, and although it is obviously not her fault, he grows more testy and complaining. In desperation she goes to the Dutchman, now employed as under-gardener on the estate. He is lying ill:

'But you *must not* die! O, you must not!' she said. And on an impulse she bent down and whispered some words to him, blushing as she had blushed in her maiden days. He replied by a faint wan smile. 'Ah—why did you not say so sooner? Time was . . . but that's past!' he said. 'I must die!'[19]

And he does.

These two groups of stories, then, form a loose association within themselves based on some common theme, attitude, or situation. It has been convenient to order

c

them in such a fashion, but it is an inescapable fact that the unifying theme of the first group could embrace all of them. Sexual deceit, faithlessness, concealment. They become almost an obsession. Yet the wry thing about it is that they rarely seem unduly forced in any given story.

In 1921, Hardy is reported to have said, "I seldom read novels now, but I understand that to-day they no longer have plots."[20] What Hardy understands by plot is most apparent in these short stories. It is an agglomeration of incident and coincident. Even the most fervid detractor could never claim that the stories lack interest, pace, readability, even if the structure of cumulative action appears at times to be monstrously involved. Yet despite this complication of manoeuvre, there is an astonishing economy in the telling: and in the stories we find the big Hardyan preoccupations as well as the commercial additives. The central theme is man: man is the story and the story is man: man, embracing woman both literally and figuratively, with his localised setting and universal problems, is presented often satirically, occasionally benignly, but always entertainingly. About man and his story are spun all those characteristic "extras," mutating from the magical to the inconsequential, but once again with the power of denying boredom: extras such as love of a countryside wearing not only its sedative importance but also its elements of hostility; the old traditions and superstitions; a gleefully morbid fascination for para-psychology and the philosophically unfamiliar; the intrusion and elaboration of architecture; the rustic dance, the church music; the sly, mischievous peeping, with a suggestion of inverted snobbery, into the country-house world of the county aristocracy; the peasant buffoonery, quaintly dialected, but always humanly and com-passionately shown. All aspects of the world of Hardy are there. Not only are the stories both illuminations and reflecting parallels of the novels and poems, they have, I repeat, the justification of themselves.

And finally, apart from a self-validity of existence, the short stories find, despite their many and extravagant incompatibilities, a resolution of unity. We have noticed a sustained concern with sexual unhappiness and the involvement of the humanly normal with the abnormally grotesque. These elements often slide together with a strange congruity. Betty Dornell,[21] emotionally cornered by maternal displeasure, kisses a girl infected with smallpox to avoid being packed off with her husband: Ella Marchmill,[22] culturally inhibited, "sleeping on a poet's lips," is spiritually seduced: the "turning" of blood: a father's transferred pride in bastardy: a milkmaid learning the fashionable polka in a country lane, as her tutor, the embodiment of an unknown hostility, stands incongruously and furtively by.[23] These stories, far from seeming outrageous or ludicrous, move into the sphere of the frighteningly plausible or, as Krishnamurti puts it, into the sphere of "freedom from the known."

## REFERENCES

1. Douglas Brown, *Thomas Hardy*, 1961, pp. 115 ff.
2. *W.T.*, pp. 286–7.
3. *C.M.*, p. 83.
4. *L.L.I.*, p. 136.
5. *C.M.*, p. 146.
6. *C.M.*, p. 167.
7. *C.M.*, p. 23.
8. *C.M.*, pp. 295–6.
9. "The Melancholy Hussar of the German Legion," *W.T.*, pp. 45 ff.
10. "Lady Mottisfont," *G.N.D.*, pp. 115 ff.
11. "The Marchioness of Stonehenge," *G.N.D.*, pp. 95 ff.
12. *W.T.*, p. 69.
13. *W.T.*, pp. 77–8.
14. *W.T.*, p. 107.
15. *G.N.D.*, p. 85.
16. *G.N.D.*, p. 90.
17. *L.L.I.*, p. 165.
18. *G.N.D.*, p. 162.
19. *G.N.D.*, p. 148.
20. V. H. Collins, *Talks with Thomas Hardy*, 1928, p. 8.
21. "The First Countess of Wessex," *G.N.D.*, pp. 3 ff.
22. "An Imaginative Woman," *L.L.I.*, pp. 3 ff.
23. "The Romantic Adventures of a Milkmaid," *C.M.*, pp. 299 ff.

# CHAPTER III

## OUTERS

The terminology of rifle shooting is used to head this and the following two chapters, to avoid the use of such controversial and arbitrary words as "failures," "unsuccessful," "minor" and so on. The novels to be considered in this chapter are on the target all right, the obvious point being that they are not *so much* on the target, but like the stories, they can contribute enormously to a bigger, more felicitous understanding of Hardy. The theme of sexual infidelity is prolifically maintained in the novels. It is not proposed to pursue this subject to the point of repetitive exhaustion but it is necessary to acknowledge it intermittently.

For the purpose of accuracy and certainty *The Poor Man and the Lady* must, I think, be ignored: the original version does not exist and in a survey of this kind there is little reward in examining the emasculated version now in print. The starting point then must be *Desperate Remedies*. Two eminent critics, who have otherwise made supremely sane and significant contributions to writings on Hardy, make observations on this novel which strike with an odd limitation today. Edmund Blunden, strangely, emphasises Hardy's skill in landscape painting:[1] and Lionel Johnson, standing almost on top of his subject, puts the novel in "the Tragic group."[2] It is tiresomely difficult to get away from the Hardy clichés. Genteel enthusiasms for his qualities as a landscape-painter serve as an anodyne for the unpleasantnesses of his darker purpose: the indiscriminate applications of labels of "Tragedy" detract from the genuine tragic moments. *Desperate Remedies* does indeed contain some close observation of the Wessex countryside and no doubt some frail elements of tragedy (although not, I suspect, where Johnson would have placed them): but there is much more besides. My complaint is not so much about what Blunden and Johnson say, but about the cursory littleness of their comment on the novel. Despite its contorted and shifting plot, high-lighting the improbable and its piling-up of coincidence, its nature of being a clumsy Victorian whodunit with Aeneas Manston the obvious criminal and the most outrageous of the Mephistopheleans,[3] the novel is immensely entertaining and readable: at times it is sincerely moving: sometimes there is delicacy and grace and felicity in its approach to solemn and subtle matters, but at other times it is overweighted with a sentimental nausea: there is some delightful and typical nonsensical stuff of romance with, however much Hardy protests, biographical flashes: it is occasionally as exciting as a modern detective story: its *comic* is stronger than its *tragic*.

The ineffectiveness of Edward Springrove, trapped both by a sense of Victorian propriety and by a set of fortuitous circumstances; the selfish pomposity of Owen Graye and the little-girl-lostness of his sister Cytherea, the early rusticana built around "Edward Springrove the elder, the landlord, now more particularly a farmer, and for two months in the year a cider-maker,"[4] the serio-comic deaths and seductions, are all typical Hardy of varying degrees of excellence. But the novel is dominated by Miss Aldclyffe and her illegitimate son Aeneas Manston. The unhealth of a thwarted spinster (if that is the proper application of the word in her case) and the consequent evil result of bottled-up pressures and of intense emotions wrongly directed, are presented with the intuition of latent mastery. Even in her moments of confession and self-revelation to Cytherea, Miss Aldclyffe mounts a frightening but authentic power. In a detailed,

remarkably frank chapter, Hardy tells how she forced
Cytherea to spend a night in her bed and A. J. Guerard
sees in this an unconscious portrayal of Lesbianism which
anticipates psychological jargon. If this is so, and
Guerard's case is ingeniously and convincingly argued,
one wonders how much such an abnormality is innate,
how much can be induced, and what is its burgeoning
potential. Certainly, at seventeen, Miss Aldclyffe's sexual
outlook appeared to be conventional. On her deathbed
she tells Cytherea of her perfectly normal young love.[5]
Whatever is the outcome of any nice analysis—and I do
not think it really matters how we define the compression
and astringency of Miss Aldclyff's emotions, so long as
we recognise their dangerous proclivities and their
astonishing authenticity—there is no doubt that Hardy
scores an early success in this portrayal of an inhibited
and frustrated woman.

The comic element in Hardy is often overlooked. I am
not referring to those contrived Dogberry-Bottom set
pieces when the bumpkins stomp together—these have a
very different value; I refer rather to that laughter, that
sense of the ludicrous which can be found in the darkest
situations. There is an exquisite example of satirical
comedy in the succession of train episodes, underscoring
the serio-clownishness of Stephen Smith and Henry
Knight, which ends in their discovery of Elfride Swancourt's coffin. Surely this is not a tragic ending to *A Pair
of Blue Eyes*, for the simple reason that Elfride's death,
however much she may have taunted and charmed us,
is not tragedy. But many of the attendant circumstances
are very much comedy—sometimes grey, sometimes wry,
admittedly, but nevertheless essentially comic. It is rarely
absent from the courting scenes: the loss of an ear-ring:
the sound of a damp kiss from the rectory garden: the
rescue of Knight from the Cliff without a Name effected
by Elfride tearing up her unmentionables—an un-
Victorian resourcefulness which reduces prudery to in-

tentioned hilarity. Even after their discovery of Elfride's death (and the last phase of her life as told later by Unity was wreathed with a rare sadness) the two unsuccessful suitors cannot withhold from their bickering as they walk from Camelton to Endelstow: their fractious quarrel about whose "darling"[6] she really was is preposterous. The anatomical probing of the essential daftness of Smith and Knight is, I am convinced, deliberate and intentional. Neither of them were from the point of view of personal qualities of very substantial account, although we have probably unwittingly and fruitlessly cheered for young Stephen.

There is a freshness and, despite some of the sadder patches, a youthful looking-forward about *A Pair of Blue Eyes*. Even if there is a little self-conscious whimsy, an obvious posturing, about the melancholy bits, they are none the less carried: not so much Elfride's death in childbirth, because, although the incident is movingly told by Unity, it is remote from us: but more in Stephen's vain vigil by the church, and, anticipating Angel Clare, in Knight's pompous rejection of Elfride. The prevailing tone, however, is sparkling: the tender fragility of young love pervades the book, and the nostalgic breezes from the Cornish coast blow through its pages: it contains Hardy's and everyman's romantic memoirs, that fleeting, unplaceable, buried time when life was young and gay. And Elfride, despite her tormenting experiences, is the everlastingly young, the provokingly unpredictable.

*The Hand of Ethelberta* is subtitled *A Comedy in Chapters*, and the odd thing is that when Hardy contrives a comedy, there are barren stretches in it which remain obstinately unfunny. He may have suspected this, for he asks for sympathetic co-operation:

.... it was given the sub-title of a comedy to indicate—though not quite accurately—the aim of the performance. A high degree of probability was not attempted in the arrangement of the incidents, and there was expected of the reader a certain lightness of mood, which should inform him with a good-natured willingness to accept the production in the spirit in which it was offered. *The characters themselves, however, were meant to be consistent and human.*[7]

Although it did perhaps appear "thirty-five years too soon," the point of start is original and bold: it is a drama, "wherein servants were as important as, or more important than, their masters; wherein the drawing-room was sketched in many cases from the point of view of the servants' hall."[7] The theme affords room for ludicrous manoeuvre, but the laughter very often holds its sides in places where it is not preordained nor expected, and the loose assortment of chapters is knit together by the developing and astonishing character of Ethelberta herself. She is, strangely enough, "consistent and human" in Hardy's sense; so, too, on different planes, are Picotee, Christopher, and Faith Julian (that stiff-lipped maintenance of dreary respectability by teaching music and living in a near-attic is so painfully accurate); and even the butler, Mr Chickerel. The same integrity in presentation cannot be granted to Lord Mountclere, Neigh, and Ladywell, although they each have their occasional moments of bleak hilarity, and the scene which involves the three of them as contesting suitors at the Hôtel Beau Séjour reaches farcical quintessence. There are, however, a harshness and sacrifice about this "comedy" which harden its outlines and reveal the Hardyan sexual bitterness in a peculiar illumination. Ethelberta is not really obliged to marry the zany Mountclere, in the same way as no girl is forced to go on the streets to endow a large family. Chickerel could have gone on butlering, Picotee pupil-teaching and spooning, and the boys were good enough mechanics. The fact is that Ethelberta's decision was calculated and unemotional: she deliberately cast aside any prospect of marital happiness, about which Hardy is sceptical anyway, and she fastened, unashamedly, avariciously, on to Mountclere. That there are and have always been willingly gullible, elderly dupes is beside the point: Ethelberta's designed victory is essentially a surrender: there is something squalid about it; it is an affront to human dignity, but paradoxically we find a strange compassion for her in her gilt-edged predicament. Despite the artificiality of her class-schizophrenia, with, as it were, one patten in the kitchen and one court-shoe in the drawing-room, Ethelberta, after one or two false starts, comes hauntingly, embarrassingly, to life: we feel her along our blood, and her place is not in situational farce.

Hardy admits that when he wrote *The Hand of Ethelberta* he was consciously seeking the bubble reputation: but it was only his intuitive and professional skill as a writer which saw him through the worst difficulties. In the first few chapters of *A Laodicean* he is once again riding serenely, although it must be remembered that *The Return of the Native* and *The Trumpet-Major* had been salutary restoratives after his venture into upper-crust farce. There are, nevertheless, conflicting elements in the early part of *A Laodicean*, and these are characteristic of the total unevenness of the novel. The quietness of a sunny August evening, against which a young architect, George Somerset, sketches the tower entrance to an English village church, is shattered by the eruption of religious controversy. The Laodicean, Paula Powers, is about to be literally immersed in the Baptist faith, but the sight of the water, either physically or spiritually, deters her. As Somerset peeps through the chapel window, he discovers a typical Hardy heroine: "which made him think that the best in woman-kind no less than the best in psalm-tunes had gone over to the Dissenters."[8] The essential indecision in the make-up of Paula is immediately revealed—an indecision which is reflected in the pace and the plot of the book as a whole. A. J. Guerard attributes the faults in structure to a succession of creative surrenders due in part to the accident that Hardy dictated most of the novel from his sickbed. The surrenders take the form of abandonments of "animating impulses."[9] There is no doubt that there are long stagnant patches; and there is no doubt, too, that after a bright start, the narrative atrophies and is not charged again until "the return of genuine comedy in Paula's absurd pursuit of Somerset through the cathedral towns and beach resorts of Normandy."[9] Apart, however, from the unpredictable and contradictory nature of Paula and the repeated efforts to reshape and revivify the story, the novel stumbles over its men characters. George Somerset is a typically docile Hardy young man: he is painfully honest, sexually correct, diffident in his approaches to courtship, where he should be forceful and dominating: he is an early, less tragically-veined, Giles Winterbourne, cheerfully passive. Captain de Stancy, melodramatically burdened with the secret of William Dare's paternity, rarely leaves the ground; and Dare himself, who begins as a study of demonic evil without human sympathies or connexions resolves into a problem bastard, a Victorian beatnik. His caddishness is very often preposterous, and the occasional laughter raised by his knavish tricks, such as the faking of Somerset's photograph, is often promoted by the wrong stimulus. Nevertheless the limp in the character-drawing is not a permanent deformity, and again there is much intentioned laughter.

There are degrees of causation of comic result, and it may be questioned whether a sure identification of the mainspring of the comedy is always necessary. Perhaps our approach to Hardy is sometimes too solemn, sometimes too finical. "There is no doubt," writes Lord David Cecil, "that, if we approach them in an irreverent spirit, we can get a great deal more fun out of Hardy's books than he ever intended."[10] I am not convinced about the lack of intention, but the fun certainly exists, and much of the value of these off-beat novels lies in just that. There has been, since its publication, virtually a unanimity of disapproval concerning *A Laodicean*, largely because, I think, fastidious hypercriticism has missed the fun. Even Lord David seems to some extent to be disappointed rather than amused by Paula's appearance in pink flannel, and cannot resist a supercilious dig at De Stancy's suddenly awakened concupiscence. Primed by Dare with a wine which was "three parts brandy " De Stancy spies into a gymnasium and watches Paula, "in a pink flannel costume . . . wheeling and undulating in the air like a gold-fish in its globe."[11] The temptation here to twentieth-century derision is almost irresistible. But surely some form of suspension of condescension is called for; surely we must appreciate, with Guerard, that "the fictional heroine or villainness who in 1870 permitted a premarital kiss must in 1915 commit adultery if she wishes to provoke the same horror in her readers; by 1945 she must be a pervert or a murderess."[12] Or to provoke the same vicarious lust. After all it is basically only the pink flannel (with its associations of stale music hall jokes) which sets us rocking: Paula, similarly cavorting in a bikini, even in 1962, could make us one with De Stancy. The fun in *A Laodicean* nevertheless exists—with a qualifying difference. Hardy is often instantaneously double-visioned: he sees simultaneously the absurd exterior and the seriousness inside:

'Will, I believe you are up to some trick,' said De Stancy, not, however, suspecting the actual truth in these unsuggestive circumstances, and with a comfortable resignation, produced by the potent liquor, *which would have been comical to an outsider,* but which, to one who had known the history and relationship of the two speakers, would have worn a sadder significance.[13]

There are two forms of inside seriousness in this pink flannel episode: there is the "sadder significance" of De Stancy's subjugation to Dare, which, like Gloucester's to Edmund, is the price of a youthful lust, and there is Hardy's earnest admiration of "Paula's presentation of herself at this moment of absolute abandonment to every muscular whim that could take possession of such a supple form."[13] What is "comical to an outsider," and to my mind intentionally so, is the ludicrous *situation* of the ageing De Stancy. Further, as is often the case, the mockery is closely associated with compassion. De Stancy is no Gloucester, but he retains, in his lickerish gullibility, a few shreds of human dignity, which we immediately and gratefully recognise.

*A Laodicean* is not a great book. It has its faults; but it has, too, its core of value. There may well be a coughing and spluttering in the mechanics of the plot; there may be irrelevant architectural reminiscence; there may be a certain mistiming of character, a dreary catalogue of a North European Cook's tour, a dated Victorianism in the matter of sexual stimulation, a preoccupation with the psychologically "unknown," which in this case falters. But there is, nevertheless, some good basic Hardy. There is that embracing capacity to perceive all the contingencies, to illuminate compassionately the dusty corners of human nature. Above all there is abundant evidence of Hardy's *intentional* sense of fun, an attribute with which, more often than not, he is perversely not credited.

*Two on a Tower* is another novel which in general receives but scant and adverse notice from the critics. It is generally recognised that it is about astronomy but that it fails in its astronomical purpose. It is true that Hardy begins the 1895 preface to the novel:

This slightly-built romance was the outcome of a wish to set the emotional history of two infinitesimal lives against the stupendous background of the stellar universe, and to impart to readers the sentiment that of these contrasting magnitudes the smaller might be the greater to them as men.[14]

He then, however, proceeds to describe popular moral reaction to publication, and how he "was made to suffer in consequence from several eminent pens"[14] which laid charges against him of impropriety and of contempt of the Established Church. In defence he maintains that "there is hardly a single caress in the book outside legal matrimony, or what was intended so to be,"[14] and that he made his Bishop "every inch a gentleman." In the event, the starry background is comparatively unimportant: it possesses a piquancy because it is unusual, and its unusual allows for the contrivance of novel and sometimes splendid situations. The morality or otherwise is neither here nor there—it is, for the most part, as Hardy insists, painfully conventional with not the slightest sign of hilarious pink flannel. And as for the Bishop of Melchester, he is one of the dullest of ecclesiastics.

The importance of *Two on a Tower* lies in the character of Lady Constantine. She is younger than Miss Aldclyffe, more attractive and more charming, but once again a study in frustration, and once again such a dominating influence that the other characters are insignificant against her. In the same preface, Hardy has no doubt about this. He hopes that a few readers "will be reminded by this imperfect story, in a manner not unprofitable to the growth of the social sympathies, of the pathos, misery, long-suffering, and divine tenderness which in real life frequently accompany the passion of such a woman as Viviette for a lover several years her junior." At the opening of the novel, Viviette, Lady Constantine, is one of the humanly lost legion of the unhappily married. She lives a sequestered and desperately lonely life in the Great House. The loneliness has been imposed by the unspeakable jealousy of her husband, Sir Blount, who to satisfy

his "mania for African lion-hunting"[15] has gone abroad:
before doing so he charges her "to avoid levity of conduct
in attending any ball, rout, or dinner"[15] to which she
might be invited: in disdainful bitterness, she volunteered
"to live like a cloistered nun during his absence."[15] She
was about twenty-eight at the time, had a warm and
affectionate nature, with something of Eustacia Vye's
domestic voluptuousness, but none of her sensual intrepidity: in this artificial plight of an unsatisfactory and
physically non-existent married state, she was "languishing for want of something to do, cherish, or suffer for."[16]
The novel is an account of her doing, cherishing, and
suffering. It is obvious that this volatile nature is near
flash-point: she is young, with normal desires, and the
mortification of such flesh cannot be unduly prolonged.
After a fairly indifferent battle with her conscience, her
emotions overspill and she falls in love with a young
Adonis, very much younger than her, a schoolboy almost.
She was bound to be the loser from the start. Nevertheless
our "social sympathies" are invoked, and we view
with trepidation the odds stacked against this forlorn
passion.

The object of her passion is Swithin St Cleeve. When
he meets the full force of Lady Constantine's sexual love
(it is first of all sexual—the cherishing, although important, is secondary), he hardly knows what the world is
about: he is more enthusiastically concerned with the
world of amateur astronomy. The outstanding thing
about him was his physical beauty—no other word can
be used—and it was this that first set Viviette's Romance
blood racing. There were, however, social status complications. Although he had been educated at Warborne
—"a place where they draw up young gam'sters' brains
like rhubarb under a ninepenny pan"[17]—he was unfortunately "linked on the maternal side with a local
agricultural family through his father's matrimonial
eccentricity."[17] Viviette faces and surmounts this diffi-

culty, and the early phases of their association have their moments of ecstasy; some of the scenes in the Rings-Hill column are indeed touched with a "divine tenderness": but even at this stage it appears that Viviette is the greater contributor to their mutual happiness, and turbulence and estrangement inevitably follow. Viviette pays with her death, not for deceiving the Bishop, but because she has transgressed against one of the subtlest but deepest rules of sophisticated social behaviour. Her movement towards middle age was in inverse proportion to the betterment and consolidation of her happiness with Swithin. When they were at last reunited after many years, she realised that: "Swithin was hopelessly her junior. Unhappily for her he had now just arrived at an age whose canon of faith it is that the silly period of woman's life is her only period of beauty. Viviette saw it all, and knew that Time had at last brought about his revenges."[18] This realisation killed her and the "pathos" and the "long-suffering" of her basically futile passion were over.

With *The Well-Beloved* we come to the last of the unfashionable books, the last of the half-dozen that receive little benediction from the critics. *The Well-Beloved* receives the least of all: A. J. Guerard writes contemptuously: "it is not the worst book ever published by a major writer. But it is certainly one of the most trivial";[19] and Douglas Brown equally unenthusiastically: "it is an original novel, certainly, but slight, and little characteristic of Hardy's gifts, and it has never been widely read."[20] Much was salvaged from the artistic defects of *Desperate Remedies* and *Two on a Tower* by the characters of Miss Aldclyffe and Lady Constantine. The same cannot be said of the central woman character of *The Well-Beloved*, partly because she is divided into three—Avice I, Avice II and Avice III— and partly because she (they) are largely symbols convenient for a preconceived notion rather than real inhabitants of the Isle of Slingers. But these inhabitants do occasionally come to life, and there are other values in the book not immediately apparent.

*The Well-Beloved* is an experiment, it is true. It is "a sketch of temperament." It was composed probably before *Jude the Obscure*, but was published afterwards, and was therefore the last of the prose fiction of novel length. Perhaps mentally and emotionally barren after the novels of the eighteen-eighties, Hardy plunges into the fanciful and pulls out of the hat the most improbable of tales. "The interest aimed at is of an ideal or subjective nature, and frankly imaginative, verisimilitude in the sequence of events has been subordinated to the said aim."[21] The subordination of verisimilitude is something of an understatement. Jocelyn Pierston, the sculptor of artistic temperament, is, through his artistic sensitiveness, a slave to a tyrannical illusion: but without this slavery, without this illusion, he would be a failure as an artist:

> To his Well-Beloved he had always been faithful; but she had had many embodiments. Each individuality known as Lucy, Jane, Flora, Evangeline, or whatnot, had been merely a transient condition of her. He did not recognize this as an excuse or as a defence, but as a fact simply. Essentially she was perhaps of no tangible substance; a spirit, a dream, a frenzy, a conception, an aroma, an epitomized sex, a light of the eye, a parting of the lips. God only knew what she really was; Pierston did not. She was indescribable.[22]

This sex-fantasy becomes incarnate from time to time and the point of the book is the human forms it takes when Pierston is twenty, forty, and sixty: it settles for these periodic phases on the women of the Caro line, all black haired beauties from the Isle of Slingers. Of the three Avice II is the most probable and most convincingly alive, despite the social distances between her and Pierston. There is the old felicitous humour of character and situation: the middle-aged sculptor turned anxious suitor of a washerwoman: the well-to-do tenant of Sylvania Castle helping her to spread out wet sheets and gallantly apprehensive that he had bruised her with a "popple": his solicitousness over her, now a servant girl, as Avice, in the kitchen of his London house, in the middle of the night, stands on a chair, frightened by a mouse: the satirical resolution of this compromising scene. There is indeed much that comes alive in the novel despite the constriction imposed by the monothematic nature of its structure.

Perhaps the most important factor about *The Well-Beloved* lies in its contrast with *Jude the Obscure*. They both stand at the end of the line of Hardy's novel-production; the one turbulent, great, with all the questions largely unanswered; the other, admittedly on a different plane altogether, spikily benevolent, showing a resigned acceptance, drained of all bitterness. There is an uneasy, *Tempest*-like tranquillity as Hardy signs off his prose, not in the stress and conflict of directionless human voyages, but, like Jocelyn Pierston, with an exhausted reconciliation. After his final sexual escapade, with all the drollness and sadness of a man of sixty courting a girl in her teens, Pierston surrenders to his young rival, becomingly begins to live and concerns himself with the philanthropic commonplace. This is a benevolently muted finale but in an overall assessment of Hardy we must listen to all the sounds. And in that perhaps lies the main value of the "outers." They are complementary, not antipathetic, to the bigger and grander stuff. There is more to be heard in them than is generally credited. In the resonance and majestic total din of Hardy's orchestration of humanity, amid its symphony and cacophony, we discern their piping tunes with pleasure.

D

## REFERENCES

1. Edmund Blunden, *op. cit.*, p. 33.
2. Lionel Johnson, *The Art of Thomas Hardy*, 1895, p. 39.
3. The expression "Mephistophelean Visitant" is originally used by Hardy to describe Diggory Venn in *The Return of the Native*: it is extended, however, to include other Hardy characters in J. O. Bailey's article, "Hardy's Mephistophelean Visitants", *PMLA*, LXI (1946): see also *A.J.G.*, pp. 96–7, where Aeneas Manston is added to the list.
4. *D.R.*, p. 139.
5. *D.R.*, pp. 441–2.
6. *P.B.E.*, p. 426.
7. *H.E.*, p. v. (my italics).
8. *L.*, p. 15.
9. *A.J.G.*, pp. 54–5.
10. Lord David Cecil, *op. cit.*, p. 127.
11. *L.*, p. 195.
12. *A.J.G.*, p. 4.
13. *L.*, p. 195. (my italics).
14. *T.T.*, p. v.
15. *T.T.*, pp. 25–6.
16. *T.T.*, p. 24.
17. *T.T.*, pp. 11–12.
18. *T.T.*, p. 311.
19. *A.J.G.*, p. 68.
20. Douglas Brown, *op. cit.*, p. 19.
21. *W.B.*, p. vi.
22. *W.B.*, pp. 10–11.

# CHAPTER IV

INNERS

This chapter is deliberately positioned, but in so placing it in the fictive scheme, I have no intention of qualitatively promoting any of the novels examined here nor of denying them literary eminence. Mine is an arbitrary judgment on them. In an upward, structural evaluation, they comprise the mid-segment of a pyramid: they rest on *A Laodicean* and *A Pair of Blue Eyes* as well as reaching up to *Tess* and *Jude*. And it is surprising how many of them have their unexpected plunges into bathos as well as achieving inspirational and imaginative splendours: but the splendidness—or something—has caught on. If previously we were concerned with books which are largely ignored and often looked upon as taboo words in the *avant-garde* critic's vocabulary, here we are concerned with novels whose growth of popularity has been consistent, despite esoteric devaluation.

*Under the Greenwood Tree*, which has probably suffered grievously through the attentions of moderators and candidates, has also probably been more widely read and more universally acclaimed than any of Hardy's novels. This is readily understandable. It is a felicitous compendium of good things, with only the faintest omens of bitterness to come. The plot is from a standard romance formula: boy meets girl: quarrel: rival: reconciliation: marriage. There is presumably happiness ever after, but the old Lucifer in Hardy twitches in the very last lines. The love-inebriated, clumsy-hearted Dick Dewy, in peasant triumph, takes home his bride "in the excellent new spring-cart," but the song of a nightingale and Dick's giddy possessiveness cause Fancy to remember "a secret she would never tell."[1] This dyspeptic conclusion to a pastoral love idyll; the slight human ugliness of deceit jarring the song of the nightingale; the hinted feminine hypocrisy and capacity for betrayal staining Dick's supreme and innocent serenity; these premature moral irritants lift the novel away from any danger of smugness or complacency about human affairs. A strange peril for Hardy this! Admittedly Fancy's was a sin of remote intent and not of commission, but nevertheless we feel that at her marriage she was less "pure," in the biggest interpretation, than Tess was when she married Angel.

There is also another sense in which the novel is down-to-earth. Apart from Fancy, who makes fluttering attempts through her schoolteacher training to rise, and Mr "Mayble," jejunely paternalistic among his rustic congregation, the action is played out in one social plane, among a hard-working people, fettered to everyday realities. The Dewy family belongs essentially to the "rustics"—although there are subtle differentials of respect, deference, and authority within the group itself—and it may be opportune, at this point, to examine cursorily a unique aspect of Hardy's writings—the rustics themselves. It is difficult to come critically fresh to them, because we have been conditioned by clichés and our path is cluttered with plausible explanation. "They are a kind of Greek chorus" and "they form the comic relief": these are the principal rehearsed responses for the secondary examinations. Guerard puts it more subtly:

> The true Hardy rustic is of *personality* all compact: of gestures, turns of phrase, humors and deformity. He has a past history, which he delights to relate, but no present history and conflict. For he is immune to suffering and change; he is part of the landscape, and his stability is a fixed screen for the rebellious and changeful protagonists.[2]

But we cannot ignore the effectiveness of choral commentary altogether, nor the element of designed comedy, for the "fixed screen" is not completely passive. There may be little physical, positive intervention in the main plot, but there is often pointed and scathing observation. Occasionally, too, there is unwitting interference with the action (there comes immediately to mind Joseph Poorgrass's delay, through a drinking bout, in bringing home the body of Fanny Robins). But, as Guerard says, they are not rounded, active protagonists in themselves—except where, as in the case of Dick Dewy, they step out of their milieu into activity and participation. They are normally human manifestations of tradition and celebration: they are the personification of old ways and superstitions and customs: they are symbolic of a peasant wariness about new doctrines and new sciences which could sweep their villages and their ways off the face of the earth.

It is interesting to notice how Dick differs from other peasant heroes and heroines. Although they are from the same class, Gabriel Oak, Giles Winterbourne, and Tess stand out from their illiterate fellows, partly, ironically enough, through the influence of an education self-pursued or government-bestowed. On the other hand, apart from his native wit, Dick is as innocent of learning as Thomas Leaf. His identity as an individual can be traced, I think, to the innate authority of his father. The other ranks have a way of sorting out instinctively their leaders which is very often more of a success than the artificial selection and inbreeding of an officer corps. Tranter Dewy is a natural sergeant-major, and the rest of the peasants of Mellstock parish are his awkward squad. Without loss of *camaraderie* or surface democracy, respect is shown unhesitatingly to his son, and this gives him the isolation from the crowd which is so artistically desirable in a central character. It must be remembered, however, that the novel is subtitled *The Mellstock Quire* and that the choir, collectively, has a centrality of character. It would seem that without any dichotomy of fictive body, Dick Dewy can be a likable young countryman with a separate identity and can also merge into the palpable human background, that agglomeration of living tradition and ancient bitter wisdom, which is at one and the same time the Mellstock choir and the rustic group of *Under the Greenwood Tree*:

'But I can sing my treble!' continued Thomas Leaf, quite delighted at being called a fool in such a friendly way; 'I can sing my treble as well as any maid, or married woman either, and better! And if Jim had lived, I should have had a clever brother! To-morrow is poor Jim's birthday. He'd ha' been twenty-six if he'd lived till to-morrow.'

'You always seem very sorry for Jim,' said old William musingly.

'Ah! I do. Such a stay to mother as he'd always have been! She'd never have had to work in her old age if he had continued strong, poor Jim!'

'What was his age when 'a died?'

'Four hours and twenty minutes, poor Jim. 'A was born as might be at night; and 'a didn't last as might be till the morning. No, 'a didn't last. Mother called en Jim on the day that would ha' been his christening-day if he had lived; and she's always thinking about en. You see he died so very young.'

'Well, 'twas rather youthful,' said Michael.

'Now to my mind that woman is very romantical on the matter o' children?' said the tranter, his eye sweeping his audience.

'Ah, well she mid be,' said Leaf. 'She had twelve regular one after another and they all, except myself, died very young; either before they was born or just afterwards.'[3]

In modern terms this could be just sick or hill-billy

humour. But under the protective shellac there is much
that is left-handedly compassionate. The repeated
abortions of Mrs Leaf were not exceptional features of
their life, and they just had to be stoically endured. In
the understatement, in the hardened but honest tolerance,
lies the philosophical adaptation and self-protection of
the peasant. The kicks must be taken, but it was useless
to kick over the traces. Life went on monotonously, but
not cheerlessly. There was an immense capacity for
enjoyment which was spontaneous and personally arrived-
at: and their social gatherings were always spiced with
macabre anecdote, wistful reminiscence—the eternal
human longing for the good old days—all washed with
the inevitable home-brewed ale or cider. Mr Robert
Penny, boot-and-shoe-maker, "a cleverer feller than
mankind in jineral";[4] Michael Mail, "a bowed and bent
man, who carried a fiddle under his arm, and walked as
if engaged in studying some subject connected with the
surface of the road";[5] Elias Spinks; Joseph Bowman; and
the idiot boy, Thomas Leaf with Wordsworthian
affinities—"a weak lath-like form trotting and stumbling
along with one shoulder forward and his head inclined to
the left, his arms dangling nervelessly in the wind as if
they were empty sleeves";[5] such idiosyncratic clowns
made their various contributions—dramatic, fey, ribald,
melancholy—to the gregarious occasions. At choir prac-
tices, there was observation of procedure and precedent:
at Christmas parties there was uninhibited, sweaty
dancing. There was no sophisticated avoidance of reality.
Close to the earth, earthiness became them. A wedding,
besides being an excuse for festivity, was frankly recognised as a necessary involvement in the process of repro-
duction.

There was, however, no third dimension to lend them
poignancy of individuality. Their cousins in *Far from the
Madding Crowd* are figures cut from the same pattern and
serve much the same purpose, but, because their choral

commentary is sung in a darker, more threatening climate, they themselves have undertones of the inimical. They reflect the universal futility and helplessness. Cainy Ball is a less daft Thomas Leaf, but in his account of his visit to Bath, where he had inadvertently seen his run-away mistress and Sergeant Troy, there is a comic exploitation of rustic innocence:

> 'And the people of Bath,' continued Cain, 'never need to light their fires except as a luxury, for the water springs up out of the earth ready boiled for use.'
> ''Tis true as the light,' testified Matthew Moon. 'I've heard other navigators say the same thing.'
> 'They drink nothing else there,' said Cain, 'and seem to enjoy it, to see how they swaller it down.'
> 'Well it seems a barbarian practice enough to us, but I daresay the natives think nothing o' it,' said Matthew.[6]

The fun of the peasant credulity is marred only by fateful circumstances behind Ball's story. Throughout the novel, there are instances of something pernicious eating into rustic integrity. The sacked Pennyways, anticipating some of the dead-beats in *Jude the Obscure*, is spiteful and rarely villainous: the farm workers succumb to Troy's authoritative blandishment at the harvest supper and in their excessive revels neglect the ricks (this sort of irresponsible toping did not happen in Mellstock): irresponsible again, Joseph Poorgrass forgets the body of Fanny Robin, lying in the mist outside the Buck's Head, as he drinks with Jan Coggan and Mark Clark, the "owners of the two most appreciative throats in the neighbourhood, within the pale of respectability."[7] Unfortunately the bounds of respectability are often broken as, at another level, human disharmony pierces the lives of the protagonists in *Far from the Madding Crowd*.

It used to be critically fashionable to regard Bathsheba as the *wronged* heroine, Oak as the stoic *hero*; two rivals,

Boldwood and Troy were, the one deadly dull and a chopping block for all the tricks of ill-chance, the other an incorrigible vagabond: the novel was satisfactorily resolved with a delayed, chastened, but happy, marriage. Lord David Cecil, postulating a Kismet-like inevitability about human affairs, removes some of the direct blame from Troy. "Fate," he writes, "often employs a human instrument to encompass the tragedies which overtake Hardy's heroines. Tess and Bathsheba, Thomasin and Grace are the victims of Don Juans."[8] If we cannot readily see what is particularly Juanish about a layabout son of a moneylender, a regular army sergeant, an impecunious innkeeper, or a hard-up doctor, perhaps we can accept the broad inference. But, to concentrate at the moment on the sergeant: Troy was simply the "human instrument," claims Lord David. R. A. Scott-James puts the matter even more tersely: "The ending is a compromise between that of tragedy and comedy. Gabriel marries Bathsheba, but not till his rivals have been tragically removed."[9] The trouble surely is that criticism tends to get bogged down with technicalities: Hardy's characters and situations are either felicitously misinterpreted or distorted to fit the Procrustean technical bed. This hawking of tragedy! This insistence on Fate and Don Juan!

The early Bathsheba is full of tomboyish charm and saucy provocativeness: the later one subdued, but with a maturer appeal: throughout, she completely wins our hearts. But ignoring Fate and human instruments and tragic compromises, there are, in the given social and moral context, elemental questions. Who philandered with Oak in the first place? Who teased Boldwood out of a contented bachelordom? Who encouraged Troy and shamelessly pursued him to Bath? The point is that Bathsheba is irresponsibly flirtatious: her mating-calls are uncontrollable and irresistible, and if she pays for this high and undiscerning sexuality, there would seem,

under her contemporary social code, to be no great injustice done. All told, she gets away with it rather lightly:
far more lightly than Eustacia, Grace, Tess, Sue. And as
for the prejudged soldier, the psychological excuses for
Troy's conduct are not necessarily all lame. It is true that
he is selfish, indulgent, limitedly promiscuous (is that a
fault or a military occupational hazard?): he is un-
thinking: within the composition of his mercurial
temperament, emotions are balanced on a knife-edge—
love can turn to contempt within an hour. But he had no
time for feminine dominance or what he might consider
to be feminine procrastination. "Treat them fairly, and
you are a lost man."[10] He is, what so many of Hardy's
heroes are not, aggressively masculine. He lived for the
sensuality of the moment: "he was a man to whom
memories were an incumbrance, and anticipations a
superfluity."[11] Yet, after all, Bathsheba damaged his life
almost as much as he damaged hers. He was prepared to
stand by Fanny Robins. He was prepared to marry her.
It was Fanny's wretched ill-luck that attendant circumstances were in such mocking contrast: as Troy waited in
vain in All Saints Church, there was giggling from the
congregation of women and girls and chuckles from
toothless old almsmen, but in his courtship of Bathsheba
there were chivalrous peacock displays of sword-drill and
romantic meetings in the hay-meads. There was a
curious warmth in the shallowness of the dandy's heart,
and an unexpected fidelity in his fickleness. As he stands
before Fanny's rough coffin, prized open by the jealous
Bathsheba, he is unequivocal and, I think, sincere:

'Ah! don't taunt me madam. This woman is more to
me, dead as she is, than ever you were, or are, or can be.
If Satan had not tempted me with that face of yours,
and those cursed coquetries, I should have married her.
I never had another thought till you came in my way.
Would to God that I had; but it is all too late! I deserve

to live in torment for this!' He turned to Fanny then. 'But never mind, darling,' he said, 'in the sight of Heaven you are my very, very wife!'[12]

Frank Troy's efforts at atonement are ludicrous, flamboyant, pathetic; but in them we can observe an induced, grotesque humility; we can arrive at a sick comprehension of the inconsiderate, and of the carnal entangled in its own inevitability. The gross pretentious headstone; the futile bundles of bulbs;[13] the malevolent symbolism of the spitting gurgoyle which washed all the plants from Fanny's grave—"this horrible stone entity was fashioned as if covered with a wrinkled hide; it had short erect ears, eyes starting from their sockets, and its fingers and hands were seizing the corners of its mouth, which they thus seemed to pull open to give free passage to the water it vomited";[14] these are all, sometimes paradoxically, emblematic of Troy's light-heartedness, his eccentric compassion, his crossed purposes: they mark the futility which was stamped early upon him.

Bathsheba's other two suitors are honest, respectable men, but in comparison with the dashing sergeant, a shade dreary—a factor which would probably make them much more easy and restful as Victorian husbands. But ever since Bathsheba's rash sending of the Valentine raised the possibility of it, Farmer Boldwood was doomed never to settle into the groove of connubial bliss. Like Angelo before he saw Isabella, Boldwood is a sexually dry stick until Miss Everdene flaunts her charms before his bewildered face. Then, the old Adam, long dormant in him, stirs. As is often the case with a prolonged repression, it develops into an obsession. Never was adolescent schoolboy so green-sick. It is one of the novel's saddest sights—this erstwhile dignified and fearfully respected farmer with his world knocked sideways by a pretty girl's whim. Yet even when his behaviour is most ridiculous, he maintains a bleak grandeur: when, in disillusionment over Bathsheba's clandestine marriage, he confesses to Gabriel that he has entirely neglected his ricks, there is a nobility of indifference, a carelessness about the materially unimportant, which place him fleetingly on heroic levels. His constitution, he claims, "is an iron one."[15] His heart, too, seems at first invulnerable: but when his heart explodes because of unpredictable pressures, the human scene is made anguishingly ragged, and few have cause for satisfaction or smugness. The innocent Oak is the uneasiest of all. It is interesting to notice in the conversation of these two rivals that he naturally calls Boldwood "sir": Gabriel Oak is a study in self-effacement and humility. This meekness of Hardy's farmer heroes is so well-rooted, and Oak has so much in common with Giles Winterbourne, that I propose to consider them together later in this chapter.

*Far from the Madding Crowd* ends, then, like *Under the Greenwood Tree*, with a pastoral wedding. There is no baleful note contrapuntal to the nightingale's song, but in their agricultural congratulations the worldly-wise bumpkins show a cynical anticipation.[16] The whole human climate of the novel is a little chillier, but the philosophy is not completely overcast. There is good humour, and many stretches of sunny pages. It is essentially a sheep and shepherd book, for which one has a deep affection, and the darker work of the main characters is played out against the frolicsomeness of malthouse gatherings, sheep shearings, harvest suppers, and Christmas parties.

The background is less frequently sunlit in *The Return of the Native*, and, to my mind, there are two unfortunate exaggerations about this novel: one is the character of Clym Yeobright and the other is the nature of Egdon Heath. Neither come to full fruition of artistry or entertainment in a deeply moving tale which has great power. With Clym, Hardy tried an experiment in characterisation. He wanted to produce a new man (complementary to the new woman?), and he turned out a dull dog. There is a dramatic build-up to his introduction, which is structurally delayed, and we anticipate a man of heroic proportions. Alas the clay of the character is refractory, and it refuses to assume a final triumphant form. Here is an intelligent rustic whose peasant ruggedness has been gold-plated by his experience in the jewellery trade in Paris, but no catalyst can be found to hasten a fusion of incompatibilities, and the native returns to his peasant superstition-bedevilled village, and there is an Aeneastic charge of glamour about him. He is virile and, to some extent, sophisticatedly moulded, although Hardy does his best to make a Frankenstein out of him. His features were unusual—"in Clym Yeobright's face could be dimly seen the typical countenance of the future."[17] No doubt to Eustacia in her first ecstasy of passion, he was strikingly handsome, but Hardy still insists on oddness: "the observer's eye was arrested, not by his face as a picture, but by his face as a page; not by what it was, but by what it recorded."[17] Of course Clym *was* odd. Surely this is an earlier masculine attempt at a Sue Bridehead. Hardy seems derisively to throw as many antipathies as possible into one personality and then watch it writhe. From the very start the inimical is postulated:

> He grew up and was helped out in life. That waggery of fate which started Clive as a writing clerk, Gay as a linen-draper, Keats as a surgeon, and a thousand others in a thousand other odd ways banished the wild and ascetic heath lad to a trade whose sole concern was with the especial symbols of self-indulgence and vainglory.[17]

The ironical thing is that this ascetic heath lad was, in an access of passion, to forget all his asceticism (which included an overall plan to do good to mankind—a sort of atonement for making diamond pendants), and to marry that very sort of woman for whom the "symbols of self-indulgence and vainglory" were made. The fact is that

Clym's vague evangelism, his martyrdom to an un-specific cause, his undefined discontent with the worldly and the fleshly, will just not be even contrivedly com-patible with his hot-bloodedness, his grand passion, his physical love for Eustacia (for indeed there was little that was ethereal about it). The picture will not hold together. At times his gormlessness cannot be credited. Having won the passionately wild Eustacia, eagerly anticipating a metropolitan and civilised life, he dumps her in the back of the beyond she hates. Having gratuitously con-tracted a disease of the eyes—and this was wretched luck indeed—he intensifies the insult to his young bride by adopting the garb and way of life of a furze-cutter, the meanest of labourers. He stretches out on the floor, like a beast, to sleep after his swink. It is under these circum-stances that Eustacia is accused of infidelity and mother-in-law murder. What is surprising is that she is not guilty of either. The "ascetic heath lad," with a boorish prodi-gality, with, in view of his Parisian background, an in-credible bush lack of delicacy, heaps indignity after in-dignity upon his new wife.

Hardy wrote novels and stories which had as their situation every corner of his nominated Wessex, and generally the changing landscapes are felicitously com-pounded into the tale. The harmony between plot and background is so prevalent that it is felt that the story could not have been told with any other geography. Tess could only have been reared in Marlott, wooed in Tal-bothays, and punished in Flintcomb-Ash: the woodlands are unobtrusively knit into *The Woodlanders*: the Isle of Slingers has Faery isolation for Jocelyn Pierston's dream-girls: and so on. But in *The Return of the Native* there is a suspicion that Hardy devised a story and then tried to hang Egdon on to it. There are, in this case, unwoven pieces. The physical geographical area known as Egdon (although for the purpose of fictive convenience it was a number of real heaths put together) undoubtedly meant

much to Hardy. He extols it in fine passages, and it would
seem that for him it existed as a personality, as a mon-
strous livingness which is more often Satanic than benevolent. People die of snake-bite on it; primitive witchcraft is practised there; there are violent drownings in
weirs; and throughout Hardy wants us to feel that the
spirit of the heath is at malicious and derisive work:

> The place became full of watchful intentness now; for
> when other things sank brooding to sleep the heath
> appeared slowly to awake and listen. Every night its
> Titanic form seemed to await something; but it had
> waited thus, unmoved, during so many centuries,
> through the crises of so many things, that it could only
> be imagined to await one last crisis—the final over-
> throw.[18]

This was a vast geomorphic devil, but it had human
assimilations:

> It was at present a place perfectly accordant with man's
> nature—neither ghastly, hateful, nor ugly: neither
> commonplace, unmeaning, nor tame; but, like man,
> slighted and enduring; and withal singularly colossal
> and mysterious in its swarthy monotony. As with some
> persons who have long lived apart, solitude seemed to
> look out of its countenance. It had a lonely face,
> suggesting tragical possibilities.[18]

The case is not that Egdon is not at times magnificently
presented. It is not that Hardy fails in conveying the
notion of threatening personalised power. It is just that
it is overdone in its "tragic possibility," in its evocation
as a protagonist in this dark love-story. A heath cannot
be a player. No amount of constriction of contingency or
arrangement of plausible incident will effect the necessary
artistic harmony. When Eustacia struggles against the
hostility of the heath, she is boxing shadows.

If, through over-complexity and too much contrivance,

Clym and Egdon are not artistically solvent, there is no doubt about the supreme success of the character of Eustacia. This queen of the night, this bundle of neuroses tingling in a body of great physical beauty, was too Shelleyean a thing for the didactic but earthbound Clym. Wildeve was paltry beside her. Her ancestry—a Corfu bandmaster's daughter—did not detract from her regality. "To be loved to madness—such was her great desire,"[19] but there was nobody mad or great enough to do so. She was ever in a spring of discontent, and one can never conjecture a phase or situation of anything like a permanent nature in which she would ever be contented. There was an insatiability about Eustacia, a restlessness, an unceasing demanding. She had to live at a hotter pace: she had to burn up quicker than anybody else. Because of her sultry grandeur, because of her disdain for the Egdon peasants, she incurred the enmity of the women especially. Mrs Yeobright considered her as good or as bad as a whore: in her prosaic eyes Eustacia is cut down to less than life size: she is "lazy and dissatisfied"; she is "that woman—a hussy."[20] Susan Nonsuch stabs her in church with a long stocking-needle, and later, as if signing her death-warrant, thrusts pins into her wax image. But the attitudes of these women, both fundamentally and for special causes, are jaundiced, and, despite them, Eustacia queens it over the Egdon she despises, and over the novel she fires. The countrified and narrow-minded pathos of Mrs Yeobright; the ancient concupiscence of Granfer Cantle, the ribald ex-serviceman of the Bang-up Locals; the long-suffering passivity of the humanly unexplained Diggory Venn, the original Mephistophelean visitant; Thomasin's Cytherea-like meekness: these are all, indeed, lively attributes of this brooding tale of applied misfortune. But its mainspring, its imaginative centrality, its energy, lie in the grand, tormented Eustacia, about whom most men would dream, but whom they would never dare to win.

Although there are some sad shades of romantic disillusion in *The Trumpet-Major*, it holds none of the
threatening gloom of *The Return of the Native*. An air of
boisterous conviviality is about. Although the darker
implications of war and military service are not ignored,
this tale of the Napoleonic Wars is burnished with military
grandeur, with the splendidness of uniform and review.
It is an adroit study of two brothers of contrasting personality and disposition; of their rivalry for the hand of a
young girl whose archness conjures unnecessary complication from the air. For the groundlings there is the
hilarious portraiture of a cowardly squire and his miserly
uncle, and the comic richness of an invasion scare in
which bewilderment, courage, and fear have modern
parallels. Although there is nothing to shock the magazine-readers (indeed much to delight them) *The Trumpet-
Major* has qualities of human analysis and perceptive
compassion which elevate it. It is controlled writing,
with a morality generally acceptable to the Victorians,
and yet at no time do we feel any stricture. Those unfortunates who people Hardy's novels are represented:
those honest failures, passive sufferers, stoic objects of the
world's scorn and ironic lashes. When proposing the injustice of the world, Hardy makes us angry with the predicament of these wooden folk of high integrity. It is the
universal soldier's lot, with its cruel inconsequence, which
marks the going of John Loveday. At his goodbyes he
pretends to Anne Garland that he is not hurt and that he
will be paying "attentions to some Spanish maid before a
month is gone by":[21] Anne, who understood him but
could never love him, is not deceived. His brother Bob,
who loved him but could never understand him, is. Bob,
with naval *insouciance*, boasts of his capture:

'It's all right, Jack, my dear fellow. After a coaxing
that would have been enough to win three ordinary
Englishwomen, five French, and ten Mulotters, she has

E

to-day agreed to bestow her hand upon me at the end of six months. Good-bye, Jack, good-bye!'

The candle held by his father shed its waving light upon John's face and uniform as with a farewell smile he turned on the doorstone, backed by the black night; and in another moment he had plunged into the darkness, the ring of his smart step dying away upon the bridge as he joined his companions-in-arms, and went off to blow his trumpet till silenced for ever upon one of the bloody battle-fields of Spain.[21]

This exit has a poignancy sharper than the Aeschylean epitaph on Tess. There is a sharp modern echo in the phrase "It's all right, Jack," but, despite the novel's concern with a populace under threat of armed invasion, there is an essential light-hearted gaiety about the book. Laughter, satirical or droll, breaks through the tense moments. Festus Derriman is superb in his equivocation on his own military valour. In his terror, he is peevishly angry that his uncle's age should shield him from combat and his bogus intrepidity is uproariously dissected as he argues that he will resist his "natural wish to rush at 'em"[22] because of the contrary tugging of his love for Anne Garland. But the satire is not savage: there is a good humour about it, a jocular if sometimes wry acceptance which is characteristic of the whole book.

With *The Woodlanders* we are aware again of a hostile intrusion, a callous indifference sporting with good men's lives. Marty South's elegiac utterance on Giles has been widely quoted, perhaps sometimes nauseatingly so, but the truth of it lies in its obviousness and in its simplicity. Giles "*was* a good man and *did* good things." He belongs to that race of the astonishingly good Hardyan characters who live in an astonishingly evil and hostile world. Apart from Marty and Tess, such characters are male, but curiously unmasculine men: not sexually perverted, but lacking in aggressiveness: in sex-conflict they are out-

manoeuvred, and their attractive women are often disappointed by their passive chivalry: a little more caddishness and assertiveness at opportune moments would
have paid dividends. They are too honourable, too self-
effacing, too long-suffering, the Edward Springroves,
Stephen Smiths, Christopher Julians, Gabriel Oaks,
John Lovedays, Giles Winterbournes—and, yes, to some
extent, the Judes. They are, often, great rocks of comfort,
stolid pillars of society, nice to have about the house, and
reassuring to grow old with. But when their women
wanted to dance, they pined for something more reck-
less, dashing, and selfish. They looked to the Manstons,
Wildeves, Fitzpiers, Troys. That they very often got what
they deserved is beside the human point. Of the good
men, two of the most virtuous are Gabriel Oak and Giles
Winterbourne, and in their alliance with two fair young
women, lifted by an incongruous refinement out of their
agricultural community, they both suffer and are scorned
for their goodness. Lascelles Abercrombie is staunch in
his admiration of their goodness:

> The steadfast lover, so faithful that personal disap-
> pointment is of no account matched with the welfare
> of the beloved, is the natural flowering here of 'plain
> heroic magnitude of mind'; of a life whose whole con-
> duct is simple unquestioning patience, a tolerant
> fortitude deeply rooted in the earth, and directly
> nourished by the imperceptible vigours of impersonal
> nature.[23]

But in his presentation of sexual relationship Hardy, I
think, is making a more involved point than this. When
he was just turned thirty, he wrote in his notebook:

> When a young woman is eager to explain her meaning
> to a lover who has carelessly, or purposely misunder-
> stood her, there is something painful to an observer
> who notices it, although it is evidence of deep love. It

somehow bespeaks that, in spite of her orders to him to
fetch and carry, of his devotion and her rule, he is in
essence the master.[24]

This is one of the notes he did not destroy when he was an
old man, and its survival may lend it maturer approval.
The paradoxical point seems to be that masculine meekness is in reality strength and authority. Bathsheba's and
Grace's victories are Pyrrhic. Gabriel and Giles were
always essentially the masters despite their continual
doffing of caps to their mistresses and their fetching and
carrying for them. Granting the equivoque of sub-
servience, Gabriel was the more subservient of the two.
Until the penultimate moment he was urging Bathsheba
to do the proper thing and marry Boldwood. There was
an occasional moment of fiery stubbornness, such as when
he refused to save the poisoned sheep until Bathsheba
stopped queening it: and there was his final moment of
triumph:

> 'And quite right, too,' said Oak. 'I've danced at your
> skittish heels, my beautiful Bathsheba, for many a long
> mile, and many a long day; and it is hard to begrudge
> me this one visit.'[25]

Nevertheless a hard fact remains: no matter how much
Gabriel is "in essence the master," Bathsheba has had
her cake and eaten it. Beside Oak, Winterbourne is no
laggard in comparison when it comes to steadfast
devotion, but he more often shows an independent spirit.
He can too be more bitter. Yet he is strangely ignorant
of the mute appeal of Marty, and there is a flaccid, in-
human martyrdom in his restraint as he lies in the wet
and cold outside the cabin he has surrendered to Grace.
Eventually, after "a dreadful enlightenment," she drags
him, dying, into the hut:

> Grace's distraction was almost as great as his. In a few
> moments she firmly believed he was dying. Unable to

withstand her impulse she knelt down beside him,
kissed his hands, and his face, and his hair, moaning in
a low voice: 'How could I! How could I!'

Her timid morality had, indeed, underrated his
chivalry till now, though she knew him so well. The
purity of his nature, his freedom from the grosser
passions, his scrupulous delicacy, had never been fully
understood by Grace till this strange self-sacrifice in
lonely juxtaposition to her own person was revealed.
The perception of it added something that was little
short of reverence to the deep affection for him of a
woman who, herself, had more of Artemis than of
Aphrodite in her constitution.[26]

The emphasis is on the value of self-discipline set within
the code of Victorian gentlemanly conduct. But in such
phrases as "freedom from the grosser passions" we get
more than a hint of the monastic constitution of these
good men who did such good things—and achieved so
little. *The Woodlanders* is the novel which, perhaps more
than any other, flays temperate feelings, abuses compassionate enthusiasms, and, almost cynically, tears
down the structures of "moral" goodness. If there is a
fault it lies in the making of the good too supine and the
amoral too superbly cocky: it is the inverse of a Victorian
fairy story. The final ironic sneer lies in the fact that not
too long after the cabin death scene, the libidinous Fitzpiers has won Grace back to him. As Marty makes her
final lonely pilgrimage to Winterbourne's grave, we
wonder who betrayed whom.

## REFERENCES

1. *U.G.T.*, p. 211.           4. *U.G.T.*, p. 20.
2. *A.J.G.*, p. 122.          5. *U.G.T.*, p. 5.
3. *U.G.T.*, p. 77.           6. *F.M.C.*, p. 253.

7. *F.M.C.*, p. 325.
8. Lord David Cecil, *op. cit.*, p. 31.
9. R. A. Scott-James, *Thomas Hardy*, 1951, p. 19.
10. *F.M.C.*, p. 193.
11. *F.M.C.*, p. 190.
12. *F.M.C.*, p. 345.
13. *F.M.C.*, p. 358.
14. *F.M.C.*, p. 361.
15. *F.M.C.*, p. 294.
16. *F.M.C.*, p. 463.
17. *R.N.*, pp. 197–9.
18. *R.N.*, pp. 4–6.
19. *R.N.*, p. 79.
20. *R.N.*, p. 228.
21. *T.M.*, p. 374.
22. *T.M.*, p. 228.
23. Lascelles Abercrombie, *Thomas Hardy*, 1919, p. 63.
24. Evelyn Hardy, *Thomas Hardy's Notebooks*, 1955, p. 29.
25. *F.M.C.*, p. 456.
26. *W.*, p. 379.

# CHAPTER V

# BULLS

There are to be found in the middle of the target (or at the top of the pyramid) three novels of vastly differing range and situation but each holding a tortuous central character who reaches (and at last we can whole-heartedly agree with Lionel Johnson and others) tragic proportions. T. R. Spivey puts it another way: "but despite being something of a meliorist and a pessimistic naturalist, Hardy the author was essentially neither. He was a writer of tragedies, a tragic poet, if you will, who did his work in prose."[1] The three works, *The Mayor of Casterbridge*, *Tess of the d'Urbervilles*, and *Jude the Obscure* have provoked in their time critical reaction varying from outright castigation to fulsome adulation. They have never bored because they *have been* so provocative. Much of the country laughter has gone. Here is a serious examination of the human condition, unflippant; a hard staring at the worst contingencies with no potential of wretchedness or ill-chance barred. The protagonists are permitted varying periods of happy respite, but for the most part they are put through the tragic mill and their lives end squalidly. If there is any fun, it is to be found mischievously sly in the corners, or harsh or derisive, mocking at *somebody's* misfortune. There is a malicious edge to the laughter occasioned by the mounting of the Skimmity ride; the boozy revelry at Rolliver's inn is far removed from the Mellstock Christmas parties: with coarse ribaldry, Arabella sniggers at feminine daintiness and masculine gullibility. But despite their unmitigated gloom, despite their depressing succession of dark accidents, thwarting at every turn any possibility of human happiness, the books are deeply moving: they have a compulsive effect like the old tragic dramas; the characters, however irritating and awkwardly embarrassing at times, come frighteningly, pathetically, sadly to life, and endear themselves. In their personal isolated struggles, they have a lonely poignancy. The world would be the poorer without Michael Henchard, for all his perverse cussedness; without Tess, despite her maddening charity; and without Jude—Jude, the saintly martyr, sporadically concupiscent and drunken.

But the comparison between dramatic tragedies and tragic novels can be overdone: there have been, to my mind, some forced comparisons between some of Hardy's characters and some of Shakespeare's. It would seem that Hardy was not too unpleased at the notion. However, to compare Henchard with Lear does an injustice to both. The thought started, presumably, because the tragic flaw (those inelastic technicalities!) is similar: that we witness the downfall of a crusty old man whom very few love. But having said these elemental things, I cannot see any essential comparison at all. Admittedly Julian Moynahan in an excellent article[2] makes a case. He refers to the comparable "conflict between generations" with Henchard belonging to one and Farfrae to the other, and this is "one of the archetypal themes" of classical Greek and Shakespearian drama. My point is that the theme is so archetypal that it is omnitypal: it is a psychological commonplace, a formula that can be applied to any popular comedian who jokes about his mother-in-law, and to many works of art on human relationships. Spivey puts it unconditionally: "there is certainly neither an Oedipus or a Lear in Hardy."[3] I must agree.

Henchard is a self-made man: he generates an enormous energy which can be utilised for the promotion of the praiseworthy or the malevolent, depending very often on which way his fortunes are running. One of the keys, I suggest, to his locked, reluctant character lies in the fact that he was starved of affection: and, like those self-made bosses of the steel-works and cotton-mills of the nineteenth century, he had no adroitness in setting about obtaining friendship and love. He thought it could be bought by the bushel. He thought he could bully it out of people. He was unceremonious in behaviour, scorned subtlety, and emotionally was a bull in a china shop. He was naturally feared, sometimes respected, and often disliked. At the top of his luck there were many who would toady, just as when cast down there were many to despise him. Unlike Oak and Winterbourne his goodness was always mutilated. Farfrae was horrified at his cavalier treatment of Abel Whittle, whom he made turn up to work without any breeches. But what Farfrae did not know was that Henchard kept Whittle's mother in winter coal, and, with a mixture of trepidation and dog-like respect, Whittle sticks to Henchard to the tawdry end. This was an ironical last affection which Henchard did not know he could command. The love that this hard man required was that of a young woman: not as a mistress, not as a wife, but as a daughter. It is true that he had an affair with Lucetta in Jersey: that with unexpected humility he compensates Susan Newson for his outrageous selling of her: that he bids desperately for the friendship of Farfrae: but what he really wanted was Elizabeth-Jane's love, the dutiful respect and affection of a daughter, who was bitterly no daughter. This very bitterness he was prepared ultimately to overlook. To keep her he was prepared to lie to her real father, uncharacteristically and in violation of his own nature.

Because by nature he was arrogantly grand, this deceit was a pettiness which did not become him: it was far meaner than the sale of his wife. But the very meanness of the act underlines the force which caused such a man to stoop so low. His self-sufficiency was draining away; the drowning, battered giant was clutching at a last emotional straw. The novel is the account of his battering by inimical and indifferent circumstances; and the strange juxtaposition of his supreme resistance to them and of his suicidal disposition to attract them. Henchard was not only a fighter of men, but of gales and storm, of intangible misadventure, of emotional forces, of himself. He was pugnaciously out of step from the start when, fired with rum, he sold his rather dull wife in the furmity booth and was puzzled by her "idiotic simplicity."[4] Until it was too late, he had no tolerance of the simple nor understanding of the meek. For the next twenty-one years he arrogantly but soberly climbed to the top of the ladder and then his years of adversity set in. His retribution is marked by the return of Susan and Elizabeth-Jane; it is intensified by an act of affection—he took a dogged fancy to the young Farfrae and bullied him into staying: it is sustained and reinvoked by his own stubbornness. Farfrae turned out to be an unwitting and to some extent unwilling cuckoo in his nest. The painstaking, placid Scotsman captures Henchard's mistress, his business, his civic eminence: and the final insult, the ultimate malignant twist of the screw which, for all his toughness, Henchard cannot endure, is when Farfrae wins his "daughter." Although this is a death-blow, he remains truculent, obstinate, defiant, clumsily affectionate until the end. The account of his last few days is poignantly told in Whittle's rustic and matter-of-fact words: he reveals, with a peasant but genuine articulation, the cause of his timid devotion to Henchard and concludes:

'We walked on like that all night; and in the blue o' the morning, when 'twas hardly day, I looked ahead o' me, and I zeed that he wambled, and could hardly drag along. By that time we had got past here, but I had seen that this house was empty as I went by, and I got him to come back; and I took down the boards from the windows, and helped him inside. "What, Whittle,"

he said, "and can ye really be such a poor fond fool as
to care for such a wretch as I!" Then I went on further,
and some neighbourly woodmen lent me a bed, and a
chair, and a few other traps, and we brought 'em here,
and made him as comfortable as we could. But he
didn't gain strength, for you see, ma'am, he couldn't
eat—no, no appetite at all—and he got weaker: and
to-day he died. One of the neighbours have gone to
get a man to measure him.'[5]

This surely is a definitive epitaph. What sticks is what
Henchard would gruffly, almost contemptuously reject.
His "kind-like" outweighs his roughness and the devotion
of this "poor fond fool" is a measure of the intense loneliness of Henchard: it marks the final social mockery in
this "story of a man of character." There remains only
the publication of his mordant pathetic will, which, with
the exception of a clause showing affectionate consideration for Elizabeth-Jane, underscores his terrible isolation,
his removal from grievous human contact, and a morbid
wish to remain so removed even after death.

This former hay-trusser dwarfs the rest of the characters. It would seem that Lucetta and Farfrae, Susan
Newson and her sailor "husband," are deliberately
muted, but, partly because she was an emotional foil
for Henchard, Elizabeth-Jane moves occasionally into
spheres of meek heroism. The setting, on the other hand,
is darkly suited to this tale of human disintegration. The
architecturally inimical is stressed; the ghosts of the long
slaughtered are conjured up: the worst features of country
traditions are emphasised, as though when country folk
come to the town, even if it is only a market town, they
become urban and evil. Mixen Lane is a far cry from
Warren's Malthouse. "Much that was sad, much that
was low, some things that were baneful, could be seen in
Mixen Lane. Vice ran freely in and out certain of the
doors of the neighbourhood. . . ."[6] Here is an absence of

peasant innocence: prostitutes in white aprons wait for "a masculine footfall along the lane,"[7] and thieves haunt the kitchens. Yet the town could be rustically gay, when the sun shone, and the crops were good, and Henchard's fortunes were at their height. There were times when Peter's Finger and its habitués could be forgotten and the air is untainted with human degradation. Then Casterbridge can show its secluded gardens, its royal occasions, its sunny rusticity:[8] but, like its stormy mayor, we are left with acuter impressions of its less favourable side. The bridge where the unfortunates loiter to stew in their own misfortune is symbolic of Casterbridge, of Michael Henchard and of the book.

With *Tess of the d'Urbervilles* we come to one of the most contentious novels in the language. Once again the theme is preposterous human suffering, an ill-starred individual, fighting the good but lonely fight against invincible odds. But this time the sufferer is an attractive peasant girl, "a pure woman" who, although she had "passed the Sixth Standard in a National School," was still a child, still a country innocent, when she was sordidly raped. Yet in *Tess*, a transcendental purity of spirit, embracing all that is charitably humble and devotedly unselfish, survived long enough to enthrone humanity in a brief splendour. The book, too, is a commentary not only on Victorian morality but on the complexity of sexual morality as a whole. Despite the martyrdom and literary canonisation of Tess, there is no vindication of unchastity, and this is a factor not necessarily forced by the magazine-readers. All Hardy's heroines are chaste—even Eustacia. Hardy, like Shaw, is remarkably fastidious when he comes to sex. Promiscuity and sluttishness are condemned. There is no fornication for its own sake, no violation of Victorian morality, in this limited sense, because Hardy professed unrestrained sexual liberty. When prescribing magazines for adult readers, Hardy writes: "Nothing in such literature should for a moment exhibit lax views of that purity of life upon which the well-being of society depends."[9] It is the harsh and indiscriminate application of a rigid morality which is resented in *Tess*. Arnold Kettle puts up a third interpretation of the novel which is eminently worthy of consideration. He argues that this is "*a roman à thèse*" and that "the thesis is true." He points out that the nineteenth century saw the culmination of the disintegration of the peasantry and the advent of capitalist farming which could have only one result:

> ... the old yeoman class of small-holders or peasants, with their traditions of independence and their own native culture, was bound to disappear. The developing forces of history were too strong for them and their way of life. And because that way of life had been proud and deep-rooted its destruction was necessarily painful and tragic. *Tess* is the story and the symbol of the destruction.[10]

That is the thesis. It is perhaps a little restricted and peremptory, but it is a truth about this novel much to be borne in mind when we are examining the humanly individual and moral aspects.

The book is built about certain centres of crisis, focal points to which there are many inrushing forces. The first and most obvious is the seduction. Our anger over this "sobbing in the Chase" is the more intense because it is presented unangrily. There is mild questioning, it is true: "where was Tess's guardian angel? where was the providence of her simple faith?"[11] There is a satiric pointing to a historical parallel: "Doubtless some of Tess d'Urberville's mailed ancestors rollicking home from a fray had dealt the same measure even more ruthlessly towards peasant girls of their time."[11] But there is no anger—only sad resignation: "As Tess's own people down in those retreats are never tired of saying among each other in their fatalistic ways: 'It was to be.' There lay the pity of it."[11] The act of human coupling is at its ugliest when it takes the form of rape, because such a barbarism is not only a violation of the woman's body, but of her personality and of her social and civilised rights. But the ugliness of d'Urberville's sin lies not only in the selfish and intemperate lust of a sexually-determined layabout: one can see other human meannesses and conditions which contributed ultimately to Alec's tawdry and comparatively easy victory. To refer back to Arnold Kettle, there was the breakdown of peasant economy, symbolised here by the accident to the Durbeyfields' horse; there was, previous to this, the boozy old Durbeyfield's acquisition of the knowledge of his ancestry and his moral blackmailing of Tess: there was Joan Durbeyfield's designed exploitation of her daughter's fresh beauty by surreptitiously marketing it; there was Tess's own nature, which, unpeasant-like, included a sexual haughtiness towards Alec which must have been for him a tantalising provocation: there was the squalid horseplay with Car Darch, "dubbed Queen of Spades, till lately a favourite of d'Urberville's,"[12] and her companions, real promiscuous sluts these. As they watch Tess gallop off with her "rescuer," their sniggering is suggestive and indicative of the dark, knowing underside of peasant innocence.[13] In the hostile climate in which Tess moved, we recognise many contributory factors besides d'Urberville's lasciviousness.

The next critical centre is the rejection of Tess by Angel Clare as they were about to go to bed on their wedding night. This iniquitous human meanness was only the inevitable culmination of the march of events and contra-distinction in character. Badness and unsuccess were written on their romance from the start. When she came to Talbothays, Tess's heart and spirit were convalescing after the insult of her seduction and the wretchedness of the death of her baby, Sorrow. It was unfair that part of the healing process should be a mad affection for Clare. She did her very best to discourage him in the foetid, sensually passionate atmosphere of that fateful summer, not because she was not desperate for human attentiveness and care, but because she was intuitively aware of the implications. In that season "when the rush of juices could almost be heard below the hiss of fertilization," when "it was impossible that the most fanciful love should not grow passionate,"[14] Tess had foreboding enough. A terror of premonition strikes her as Dairyman Crick tells Clare the story of "Jack Dollop, a 'hore's-bird of a fellow we had here," who "courted a young woman over at Mellstock, and deceived her as he had deceived many afore."[15] She tries again and again to tell Angel her history, but it always sticks in her throat at the last minute, either through accident, embarrassment, or jealousy. One tends to forget Tess's unquenchable spirit, which is at times identifiable with her determination: despite her essential femininity and youthfulness, there is a hard will. Perhaps with an unforeseen and immeasurable chance of happiness before her, she never really meant to let Clare go: she was certainly not going to surrender him to such throbbing countrified hearts as those of Marian, Retty Priddle or Izz Huett:

'I shall give way—I shall say yes—I shall let myself marry him—I cannot help it!' she jealously panted, with her hot face to the pillow that night, on hearing one of the other girls sigh his name in her sleep. I can't bear to let anybody have him but me!'[16]

Unsuitability is woven into the character of Angel Clare. He has an eccentricity of heritage, and there is instability about his one-eyed idealism, about his emotional intrusion into a socially lower, alien world, which threatens immediately his future marriage with Tess. He has a history of philosophical vacillation: his vague but curiously limited inquiries clash with the lifeless hide-bound puritanism of his parents. His mother's reaction to Mrs Crick's gift is tight-lipped: "I found the

mead so extremely alcoholic that it was quite unfit for
use as a beverage, but as valuable as rum and brandy in
an emergency; so I have put it in my medicine-closet."[17]
His father echoes the act with the dogma: "We never
drink spirits at this table, on principle."[17] This is no
specious defence of Clare, but it must be remembered
that he had the energy, however sloppily directed, to
break away from his Low-Church restrictions, from the
Sunday-school primness of Mercy Chant, from the
officious tendentiousness of his brothers. It was part of
the inimical and the inevitable that his adventuring
from his social class involved him and his wife in disaster.
However squalid his rejection of Tess was, and we have
nothing but contempt for him during that evening of
masochistic preaching when he sickenly parades his
injured ego, we must realise that Clare was just as much
a victim of circumstantial morality as Tess. The difference
is that it hurts us more to see Tess suffer.

The exact positioning of the final and tragic point of
the novel is a matter for some conjecture. It could be
looked upon *serially* as a shifting focus of crisis. It certainly
begins or comes to one head in Kingsbere Church, when
Tess, only too conscious of her wretched family camped
outside, obviously makes her agonising decision to deny
her marriage and go to live with d'Urberville. She simply
has no more resistance, but it is important to notice that
it was not her own suffering that was unbearable, but the
suffering and predicament of her supine mother and of
the children to whom she was so attached. In this she is at
once similar and dissimilar to Henchard. He cries out
petulantly in his will. She cries piteously outside the
d'Urberville burial vaults, "Why am I on the wrong side
of this door!"[18] Although it is nowhere specifically
stated, this is the moment one imagines that she decides
on her inglorious surrender: and the squalidness of it
must have been more intense to Tess than to anyone else.
She could, however, not be left alone in her moral capitu-

lation, to which no doubt in time she would have become passively hardened and indifferent. There must be a re-visitation of irony. The reappearance of the repentant Clare at the Bournemouth boarding-house marks the penultimate crisis and emphasises for Tess both her self-revulsion and the enormousness of the marital happiness that had escaped her. Tess had a practical peasant answer to a situation that was now emotionally and morally un-tenable. She and Alec had been about to breakfast in their room: Tess was still in her embroidered nightgown (a garment emblematically shameful as it is with Sue Bridehead?): she was hysterically upbraiding d'Urber-ville and at a dirty word from him she killed him, like a pig, with the carving-knife. The killing was entirely with-out any feeling for d'Urberville: it was an act of recon-ciliation through which she would move back to the serenity of Angel Clare's love:

'I never loved him at all, Angel, as I loved you. You know it, don't you? You believe it? You didn't come back to me, and I was obliged to go back to him. Why did you go away—why did you—when I loved you so? I can't think why you did it. But I don't blame you, only, Angel, will you forgive me my sin against you, now I have killed him? I thought as I ran along that you would be sure to forgive me now I have done that. It came to me as a shining light that I should get you back that way. I could not bear the loss of you any longer—you don't know how entirely I was unable to bear your not loving me! Say you do now, dear, dear husband; say you do now, now I have killed him!'[19]

An accepted placing of the final catastrophe is on those pages which describe the Stonehenge sleep and the execution at Winchester; this is preceded by a serene, if cloudland, interlude when Tess's marriage is at last con-summated in an empty house at Bramshurst. This quasi-happy phase may well have been subconsciously to

F

placate the outraged sentiments of the magazine-readers, but the artistic end of the book is surely at the point of Clare's reappearance, when the "shining light" comes to the sullied, morally besmirched Tess, and she kills Alec d'Urberville without compunction. That was the pathetically magnificent end: that was the completion of an unpretentious but gallant soul's expiation.

Hardy puts his final concentration of bitterness into *Jude the Obscure*. There is no tempering with mercy or compassion, no Chorus of Pities to say a prayer of alleviation for the chief characters. There must have been a number of years during which Jude and Sue lived together with a certain amount of conjugal bliss, but these years are fictively skipped. Once again it is the story of a lonely individual involved in a personal terrible struggle, but, in this case, much of Jude Fawley's fight is with himself: there is a constant conflict between his bright-eyed idealism and his grosser desires. Sue Bridehead, who wavers between the sexual attitudes of a normal child-bearing mother and those of the "new woman," with her bachelor-girl independence and epicene tendencies, has within her own complex make-up an unresolved conflict which has a parallel with Jude's but is essentially different. With the dry propriety and incompatibility of Phillotson and the fecund amiability of Arabella in the background, Jude and Sue are involved in a sexual struggle during the course of which both are very badly hurt, and during which the whole complexity of moral canons is taken to pieces. And all is written in a spirit of great bitterness as though defiance were being hurled into the teeth of uncompromising hostility. All the country laughter has gone.

There are four factors about Jude which call for attention. Like the young Hardy, he was filled with academic ambition, a desire for learning for learning's sake, which can be identified with his "idealism," and, like the young Hardy, he set about his self-teaching infinitely laboriously, and with great persistence and determination. Unlike the young Hardy—as far as we know—this ambition could be easily unseated through his voluptuous propensities. The next two factors concern this voluptuousness and are at once antagonistic and complementary. A *nostalgie de boue* was stronger in Jude than in most men: it can perhaps be associated with Henchard's self-destructivism: with Jude it most often took the form of a sensual wallowing with Arabella. Contrapuntal to this was his elevation of purity to a Sue Bridehead pedestal, a roseate idealisation of sexual relationship, which did not, however, necessarily exclude the physical aspects. Finally there were sporadic descents into alcoholic anaesthesia on those occasions when the game became too much for him.

Jude's seduction, like Tess's, has a centrality of importance, but it arises for very different reasons; here there is no piling-up of malignant outside forces and ill chance. Apart from the *existence* of Arabella, there is no-one to blame for Jude's seduction but his own lustful self. He desired and got this "fine dark-eyed girl," who had 'a round and prominent bosom, full lips, perfect teeth, and the rich complexion of a Cochin hen's egg," and who 'was a complete and substantial female animal—no more, no less."[20] There is, of course, no doubt that Arabella was the enticing agent. From the moment that Jude was hit in the ear, symbolically, by "a piece of flesh, the characteristic part of a barrow-pig, which the countrymen used for greasing their boots,"[21] he was controlled by his loins. Arabella exploited her feminine lure with intuitive wit, but she did so with contemptuous ease, and the sad thing is Jude's gullibility. Their association was diseased with contempt: Arabella's for Jude's finer instincts and Jude's for her animal and coarse ones. Unfortunately whilst Arabella could never be refined, Jude could be governed by his gross impulses. Norman Holland Jr notices the sad parallelisms: "No matter with whom Jude and Sue settle, a mismatch is inevitable. They both aspire to some form of higher life, whereas Arabella and Phillotson seek only suitable social niches."[22] One could add that Arabella's "suitable social niche" involved a fleshly allure which Jude found irresistible: the first and disastrous seduction, where he ruined his highminded plans for Oxford, because he rushed upstairs at the heels of the buxom daughter of a shiftless pig-farmer, was not the only one: the lesson, bitter as it was, was not fully learned. There was another night in a third-rate inn in Aldbrickham which paradoxically pained Sue so much when she learned about it.

But then Sue's relationship with Jude was full of paradox. She is not the normal country heroine, but is reasonably intellectual, and is unparochial. She is obviously attractive, with becoming ways and feminine daintiness, and it is not surprising that Jude fell in love with her. But she is full of sexual contradictions, and at times her behaviour is neurotically unexpected. Her aunt detected the complications at an early age. She was "a pert little thing with tight-strained nerves":[23] she lifted her dress to show her legs and then impertinently commented to her aunt, "Move on, aunty! This is no sight for modest eyes!"[23] She blew flirtatiously hot and cold with the village lads sliding on the pond. Her frigidity is at its most remarkable during the period she lived with a Christminster graduate for fifteen months and repulsed all his advances: her belief was that "no average man—no man short of a sensual savage—will molest a woman by night or day, at home or abroad, unless she invites him."[24] But she was also aware, and she tells the story with a mixture of pride and shame, that she caused the death of the Christminster man through what A. J. Guerard calls her "epicene reticence." Her marriage with Phillotson was essentially to spite Jude after he had confessed "the episode in my life which brought about the marriage."[25] The unfortunate Phillotson was such a

repulsive scarecrow that Sue could be forgiven for jump-
ing out of the window when he enters her bedroom, but
the act is typical of her vacillating emotions, and it cannot all be attributed to her plea that "Our family have
been unlucky of late years in choosing mates."[26] These,
then, were some of the oddnesses of her sexual history
when she eloped with Jude, and surely we expect, as he
certainly does, that the moment of surrender and normalcy has arrived. But this exasperating, delightful
creature parries still further. As they run away in the
train she asks about accommodation and is horrified to
learn that Jude has booked only one room. Jude's con-
sternation at this reaction is very understandable and he
is not appreciative of her excuse:

> Even at this obvious moment for candour Sue could
> not be quite candid as to the state of that mystery, her
> heart. 'Put it down to my timidity,' she said with
> hurried evasiveness; 'to a woman's natural timidity
> when the crisis comes. I *may* feel as well as you that I
> have a perfect right to live with you as you thought—
> from this moment. I *may* hold the opinion that, in a
> proper state of society, the father of a woman's child
> will be as much a private matter of hers as the cut of
> her under-linen, on whom nobody will have any right
> to question her. But partly, perhaps, because it is by
> his generosity that I am now free, I would rather not be
> other than a little rigid. If there had been a rope-ladder,
> and he had run after us with pistols, it would have
> seemed different, and I may have acted otherwise. But
> don't press me and criticize me, Jude! Assume that I
> haven't the courage of my opinions.'[27]

Hardy, rather than use psychological jargon, attributes
Sue's complexities to "that mystery, her heart." But such
was her vexed temperament, and such was Jude's, that to
bring them in contact was to set loose all the tragic poten-
tials. Disharmony was inevitable. Domesticity could

never settle on so highly volatile personalities. They tried it for a time and had children just like any other couple. This happy time was shattered by the Mephisthophelean antics of a grotesque gnome, but one feels that the happy time was very transient anyway. Father Time, pathetically worldly-wise, older and meaner than Tess's Sorrow, but symbolically akin, is evocative of Jude's early folly. But in the killing of their children, "*Done because we are too menny*,"[28] there is a greater badness, a badness which tainted the whole of the relationship between Jude and Sue. From this point, events raced into their final sad turbulence. Sue, deranged by grief, was self-mesmerised into a curious act of contrition, what Jude called "a fanatic prostitution,"[29] and returned to Phillotson. This time, clenching her teeth and closing her eyes, she surrendered to him physically. This act may be more tragic than Jude's death. He, like Tess Durbeyfield and Michael Henchard, was to die in squalid circumstances. Having been trapped by liquor, he is idealistically bitter. To Arabella, whom he is about to re-wed, he declares, "I'd marry the W— of Babylon rather than do anything dishonourable."[30] But his death is more from a despondent heart than congested lungs and comes after he learns of Sue's betrayal of herself to convention. Henchard-like he is Scripturally defiant on his deathbed:

'*Let the day perish wherein I was born, and the night in which it was said, There is a man child conceived.*'[31]

*Jude the Obscure* is the grimmest and most poignant of the three great novels, but it is elevated by a human attachment, which, however doomed, incompatible and maladjusted it was, reached an unbearable intensity and a paradoxical permanence. In her heart of hearts the earthy Arabella knew this. Mrs Edlin, endeavouring to wrap things in the consolatory commonplace, declares that Sue has found peace:

'She may swear that on her knees to the holy cross upon her necklace till she's hoarse, but it won't be true!' said Arabella. 'She's never found peace since she left his arms, and never will again till she's as he is now!'[32]

## REFERENCES

1. Ted R. Spivey, "Thomas Hardy's Tragic Hero," in *Nineteenth Century Fiction*, Vol. IX (1954), p. 181.
2. Julian Moynahan, "*The Mayor of Casterbridge* and the Old Testament's First Book of Samuel: A Study of some Literary Relationships," in *PMLA*, Vol. LXXI, No. 1. (1956), pp. 118–130.
3. Ted. R. Spivey, *op. cit.*, p. 182.
4. *M.C.*, p. 17.
5. *M.C.*, p. 383.
6. *M.C.*, p. 293.
7. *M.C.*, p. 295.
8. *M.C.*, p. 65.
9. Thomas Hardy, "Candour in English Fiction," in *The New Review* Vol. II. No. 8. (1890), p. 21.
10. Arnold Kettle, *An Introduction to the English Novel*, Vol. II. (1961) p. 49.
11. *T.D.*, p. 91.
12. *T.D.*, p. 80.
13. *T.D.*, p. 84.
14. *T.D.*, p. 190.
15. *T.D.*, p. 171.
16. *T.D.*, p. 229.
17. *T.D.*, p. 207.
18. *T.D.*, p. 465.
19. *T.D.*, pp. 491–2.
20. *J.O.*, p. 42.
21. *J.O.*, p. 41.
22. Norman Holland, "*Jude the Obscure*: Hardy's Symbolic Indictment of Christianity," in *Nineteenth Century Fiction*, Vol. IX (1954), p. 52.
23. *J.O.*, p. 131.
24. *J.O.*, p. 177.
25. *J.O.*, p. 199.
26. *J.O.*, p. 201.
27. *J.O.*, pp. 287–8.
28. *J.O.*, p. 405.
29. *J.O.*, p. 436.
30. *J.O.*, p. 461.
31. *J.O.*, p. 488.
32. *J.O.*, p. 494.

# CHAPTER VI

# THE WINTRY HARVEST[1]

In 1922 V. H. Collins proposed an English translation of F. A. Hedgcock's *Thomas Hardy: Penseur et Artiste* which had been published by Hachette. In a discussion on the book, Hardy is reported to have said: "As the book is ten years old it is of course out of proportion, for I have now written verse for twenty-seven years and prose only twenty-five."[2] This was no doubt largely tea-time chatter, uttered with no profound deliberation; and it is not suggested that Hardy considered seriously that a critical review should be quantitatively proportioned relative to the number of years spent on either species of creative writing. However, Hardy preferred to be thought of as a poet, and placed at least as much value on his poetry as on his prose fiction, and if, in his view, Hedgcock's work is out of proportion, this one is too. There is no defence other than that of a predisposition and of a conviction that there has been a recent gross underestimating of the importance of Hardy's prose fiction. For all this it is accepted that the poetry has an eminent and noble place.

*The Dynasts* is more of the nature of poetry than of drama. Although the work is set out in the conventional form for stage presentation, it must be recognised that, in 1903 at any rate, Hardy did not visualise any such presentation and stated that it was "intended simply for mental performance, and not for the stage."[3] It is indeed a painting in dramatic form of an historical panorama of "a vast international tragedy."[4] It is authoritatively declared and sustained with industrious research. There is no denying the splendidness of its conception and the boldness of its plan with its "three parts, nineteen acts, and one hundred and thirty scenes." The canvas is crowded in this "historical presentment on an intermittent plan, in which the *dramatis personae* number some hundreds, exclusive of crowds and armies."[5] Regrettably there is all the difference between splendour of speculative plan and incisiveness of execution; between execution and resultant artistic effect. Hardy lamented that in *The Trumpet-Major* he touched only the fringe of a theme of vast creative possibility. But *The Trumpet-Major* is more humanly compulsive, artistically unified, of integrity. In *The Dynasts* Hardy is dealing on a wide screen with the immensity of spectacle, and forgets, what in his prose he interprets so felicitously, the immensity of humanity.

We must accept Hardy's protest that the Phantom Intelligences of the Overworld were "contrivances of fancy merely" and that "their doctrines are but tentative, and are advanced with little eye to a systematised philosophy."[6] But even if it is not systematised, an essential part of the philosophy of *The Dynasts* is the proposal of an eternal indifference, what Hardy calls the Immanent Will. A complex machinery of the extra-sensory is superimposed on the human vistas, and it caustically records, observes, hardly ever interferes in, human destiny: it interprets the workings, or the non-workings, of the Immanence. This machinery appears as impersonated abstractions under such guises as the Shades of the Earth, the Spirit of the Years, the Chorus of Pities (the only one, Hardy tells us in the Preface, to approximate to the classical Greek chorus, to Schlegel's "Universal Sympathy of human nature—the spectator idealized"),[7] the Spirit Ironic, the Semichorus of Rumours, and, incongruously, a Recording Angel. This extra-terrene galaxy had to be used, the author claims, because the "Monistic theory of the Universe in this twentieth-century" excluded other, more readily recognisable, arrays of gods. For this reason the classical divinities were out as was the Miltonic

spiritual upper crust. But the utterances of these intel-
lectualised essences are indeed often of the stuff of poetry
and thought. The epic begins with a speculative indica-
tion of the Immanent Will, with its listless threat:

### SPIRIT OF THE YEARS

It works unconsciously, as heretofore,
Eternal artistries in Circumstance,
Whose patterns, wrought by rapt aesthetic rote,
Seem in themselves Its single listless aim,
And not their consequence.[8]

and ends, one hundred and twenty-nine scenes later,
with echoes even more inimical:

### SPIRIT OF THE YEARS

Thus doth the Great Foresightless mechanize
In blank entrancement now as evermore
Its ceaseless artistries in Circumstance
Of curious stuff and braid, as just forthshown.
Yet but one flimsy riband of Its web
Have we here watched in weaving—web Enorm,
Whose furthest hem and selvage may extend
To where the roars and plashings of the flames
Of earth-invisible suns swell noisily,
And onwards into ghastly gulfs of sky,
Where hideous presences churn through the dark—
Monsters of magnitude without a shape,
Hanging amid deep wells of nothingness.[9]

This brings us to the main importance of *The Dynasts*.
Despite some dreary scenes (because Hardy will leave
nothing out) such as those Parliamentary debates,
Napoleonic rhetoric, and Pitt's frustrating policy talks
with George, the epic is lit with flashes of isolated splendour and sustained with an intricacy of thought. If we
can forget the artificiality of the Spirit of the Years, sitting

judicially, as it were, in the front row of the celestial stalls, the lines just quoted on monistic callousness have an intrinsic meditativeness of their own, a sad concern with human futility, which touches morbid greatness. At this point, without doing anything like justice to it, one cannot ignore J. O. Bailey's scholarly and informed interpretation.[10] He sees *The Dynasts*, philosophically, not as illustrating Schopenhauer's pessimism, but as a positive progress of evolutionary meliorism:

> Men gained cognition with the flux of time,
> And wherefore not the Force informing them. . . .[11]

There are two possible stages in dispersing the neutrality of the Immanent Will: "The first of the stages is awareness, the breaking of blindness";[12] and later comes: "the waking of the heart—the development of compassion as a consequence of awareness."[12]

But, less abstrusely, though with a surer mastery, Hardy gives us passages, shot with a Wessex nostalgia, when the captains and the kings—and, could it be, those slightly ridiculous phantom intelligences—are forgotten, and he deals with the common men, the soldiers, the boatmen, the prostitutes, the First and Second Pedestrians, and once again we associate him with more readily identifiable human comprehension. There is the eternal soldier's eternal longing for peace in the midst of war: there is familiar military sexual reminiscence. On the eve of battle on the plain of Vitoria, we are in a universal army of all time:

### THIRD HUSSAR

You walked with a girl there for some weeks, Sergeant, if my memory serves?

### SERGEANT YOUNG

I did. And a pretty girl 'a was. But nothing came on't. A month afore we struck camp she married a tallow-

chandler's dipper of Little Nicholas Lane. I was a good
deal upset about it at the time. But one gets over
things!

### Second Hussar

'Twas a low taste in the hussy, come to that.—How-
somever, I agree about Budmouth.[13]

As they wait to be wiped out or mutilated they sing of the
"Budmouth Dears" and dream salaciously of arch girls
in muslin gowns. This may be the Immanent Will at
work—or not at work—but the grim situation is threaded
with compassion and understanding.

Hardy can, indeed, with a god's eye view, provide the
scenic voids, the massive landscapes and seascapes against
which his particular "flimsy riband" of the "web
Enorm" is to be played. There are no doubt epic aspects:
the thematic bigness—the Napoleonic Wars between
1805 and 1815: the wide Continental stage: the involvement of all time and all philosophy with the spiritualisa-
tion of forces which are supra-humanity. But, for all this,
artistic unity has not been realised, because there has
been too much conscious effort at co-ordination—as if
Hardy were planning a world cut to his own orthodoxy—
a curious orthodoxy, as indeed Bailey suggests, but an
insistent one. There are phases of high achievement in
*The Dynasts*, but the artificiality of the design, the very
lack of cohesion, prevent the communication coming
over all of a piece. R. A. Scott-James contends that *The
Dynasts* is the "finale of a great body of work,"[14] but there
is no doubt in my mind that Hardy's world is presented
more effectively in his prose fiction: that *The Dynasts*, far
from being a successful culmination, sounds only faint
artistic echoes of what was done so magnificently and
compassionately in the novels and stories. The epic
drama has become a museum piece; a fascinating area
for the erudite investigator, but artistically more dead
than alive.

Although *The Dynasts* contains some meditative and lyric poetry of a high order, Hardy's essential poetic force and inspiration are to be found, naturally, in the *Collected Poems*. He wrote near to a thousand, most of them, but by no means all, after he had completed his prose fiction writing. In other words, from his fifties onwards. As Young puts it, "This ancient music? This gnarled and wintry phrasing?"[15] But the ancient could occasionally attune his songs to springtime, to young love and pastoral romance; and, although they are often clouded by the pain of knowledge that such days and moods are unreturnable, they contain a livingness of sad serenity; in some cases, inevitably, the recollected emotion is much more ecstatic than the original reality: memory and temporal distance lend enchantment. This is, perhaps, particularly true of the elegiac pieces on Emma. But there is too, savagery on the sexual theme, as well as romantic illusion: the familiar sinister rears its inimical head, in balladic stories of betrayed and deserted countrywomen. The peasants of "Time's Laughingstocks" are drawn from harsh village reality, not from Elysian fields "under the greenwood tree." We discover, among the thousand, the never quenchable love of music, both church and lay, and of dance and village festivity; of folk-lore and tradition; there is the raising of the strange, the eerie, the disturbingly abnormal; fairs and markets, funerals and weddings, soldiers and wars; many are backed with those essential Wessex countryside features, sometimes sunny in Maytime, sometimes autumnal and wintrily bleak; and some are twisted by the inimical indifference to human affairs, that callousness which Hardy defined in *The Dynasts* as the "Great Foresightless" or the Immanent Will. Technically the poems show, naturally, varied accomplishment but there is a constant experiment with metre and verse form. There is inevitably some trite versification, but the triteness is not, I suggest, as wide-spread as F. R. Leavis claims: commenting on the small proportion of great poems in Hardy's work he writes:

> How small a proportion this is does not seem to be generally recognized: his rank as a major poet rests upon a dozen poems. These are lost among a vast bulk of verse interesting only by its oddity and idiosyncrasy. . . .[16]

From this formidable collection of poems then, including the "odd" and the "idiosyncratic," pieces for particular consideration must be arbitrarily selected. There must be vast omissions. *The Wessex Poems*, the first of the volumes of collections, was published in 1898 and contained pieces written over the previous thirty years. Only four had been published before. Many must have coincided, in initial conception at least, with the time of the great creative bursts of the fiction writing. "The pieces are in a large degree dramatic or personative in conception," Hardy writes in the Preface.[17] This is obviously true. Many of them have plots which could form the basis of an anecdote, a story, or even a novel and many have a characterisation which is rounded and vital. The early love poems "Amabel," "Postponement," "Neutral Tones," "Her Dilemma," "She to Him," to isolate a few of them, have a melancholic distortion of a potential happiness which may be a "personative" recollection of an actual crossed affair, or may simply be the "romantic" outpourings of an introspective young man, poetically, but naturally Acherontically, disposed. A stanza from "Neutral Tones" is characteristic of this youthfully morbid phase:

> The smile on your mouth was the deadest thing
> Alive enough to have strength to die;
> And a grin of bitterness swept thereby
>     Like an ominous bird a-wing. . . .[18]

There was, too, an early preoccupation with violence, faithlessness and disillusionment. The betrayal theme of the short stories is discovered in "San Sebastion," in which a sergeant's guilt has so burned his soul that he was denied happiness in retirement, and pleasure in the maturing of his comely daughter. Retribution can be harvested in untranquillity; the mind can be permanently deformed by its lack of peace. After the storming of San Sebastian, the sergeant had, "with the fire of the wine alight," raped a young Spanish girl. With one of those abnormal transferences, which so intrigued Hardy, he had perpetuated the "beseeching eyes" of the ravished girl, through the act of begetting, in his own daughter, so that his own blood became a living remonstrance for his lust, a "God-set brand like Cain's." The old soldier, incapable of being shriven, unconsoled by past military glory, everlastingly poisoned by his shame, laments to his anonymous questioner:

> "And I nightly stray on the Ivel Way
> As though at home there were spectres rife;
> I delight me not in my proud career;
> And 'tis coals of fire that a gracious wife
> Should have brought me a daughter dear!"[19]

"The Peasant's Confession" also recalls the Napoleonic Wars. In a fanciful reconstruction, where an indiscriminate, seemingly insignificant, act of a countryman affects the destiny of nations, the intransigent haunting of a guilty deed of violence is once more the theme.[20] Disillusion and, later, hallucination sustain the balladic "My Cicely,"[21] and again a barely credible quirk in human nature is examined. A lover gallops to what he misguidedly thinks is the funeral of his lady, Cicely. On discovering that the dead one is not Cicely, he is at first ecstatic with relief, only to be downcast again when he learns that Cicely has married a lackey from a stage-hostel, the Three Lions; that in her social descent her personality has disintegrated—a familiar Hardy theme this; he observes "her jests with the tapsters" and "her liquor-fired face." In his distress, there is achieved a sublimation of his affections by a substitution of the object of them: his emotions are irrationally redirected; and although he is accused of being "frail-witted and illuded," he develops a deep and apparently genuine love for the unknown buried woman. It goes further than this. The unknown is eventually identified, in his mind with the original, undefiled Cicely.

*Poems of the Past and the Present* (1901) contained a number of poems previously published in journals and magazines. In the *War Poems* of this volume, there is a movement away from the overlaid glamour and swagger which burnished the rancour of the Napoleonic Wars, towards a more modern horror and sickening apprehension of war. The timorous sadness of separation is caught in the couplet:

> Wives, sisters, parents, wave white hands and smile,
> As if they knew not that they weep the while.[22]

In "The Colonel's Soliloquy," the ageing veteran commander, losing with his youth its vitality and hopefulness, detects a self-directed mockery in the playing of "The Girl I've left behind me," the more so when the girl he has left behind is a grandmother.[23] Wives lament in "The Going of the Battery,"[24] and one detects a note of familiar flat dismay, which the cold formality of the casualty lists brings, in "At the War Office, London."[25] "The Coquette and After," a poem of sixteen lines, which is masterly in bitter compression, is a return to more traditional Hardy. There is a certain illumination here on the complexity of Hardy's thinking on moral outlawry. The conclusion of the piece:

> .... Of sinners two
> At last *one* pays the penalty—
> The woman—women always do![26]

suggests something of the harsh application of social laws as applied to Tess. Yet the first stanza is so emotionally designed to propose that retribution could be anticipated, was inevitable, and carried to some extent a rough justice.

Hardy's concern with the minutiae of the countryside (which very often, however, is related to the greater tawdriness and futility of mankind) is in evidence in the two thrush poems. "The Darkling Thrush" is reasonably well known and is favoured by the anthologies, but there is a remarkable Wordsworthian flavour both thematically and philosophically about "The Caged Thrush Freed and Home Again" which is rare in Hardy's poetry. Despite a declared imitation of the French villanelle form, there is more of the Lake District in its diction and sense. After the five three-line stanzas, with their rime limitation, the refrain "How happy days are made to be," leads into the final quatrain:

> "Eludes great Man's sagacity
> No less than ours, O tribes in treen!
> Men know but little more than we
> How happy days are made to be."[27]

Hardy belongs to no particular poetic coterie: he is neither at the end of one nor the beginning of one, but we discern occasional echoes of nineteenth-century poets.

*Time's Laughingstocks and Other Verses* was published in 1909, but Hardy reminds us that the pieces were "written at widely severed dates, and in contrasting moods and circumstances." There are fifteen poems under the section —and how viciously apt is its title—*Time's Laughingstocks*: they represent some of Hardy's most pungent and powerful verses: powerful, that is, in *concentration* of force: they are comparable in their emotional antagonisms with the worst bitternesses of the prose fiction, but the space for manoeuvre in the latter sometimes allows a fitful geniality to settle. "The Revisitation" is concerned with that recurring theme of the impermanence of woman's beauty, with the disastrous effects of "Time's transforming chisel," and concludes with the bleak line of resignation: "Love is lame at fifty years."[28] The nature of a repentant coquette is recalled in "A Trampwoman's Tragedy" but this time, in the shape of a dramatic monologue, a peasant tale of sudden violence is told in more detail: there is a probing into the remorse of a woman hobo, morally carefree and flirtatiously vexing. After her fancy-man had been hanged because of her provocation, there is a curiously moving coda in which she protests to his ghost that, since her association with him at any rate, she had "kept me from all men."[29] Time and again we come across the existence of a strict peasant social code from which any deviation is severely punished. That peasants do commit sins of venery, quite frequently, is recognised, but they move in a harsh retributive climate. The unfortunate mother from Pydel Vale in "A Sunday Morning Tragedy" induces guilt because she transgresses natural laws in a desperate bid to camouflage her daughter's carelessness. She tries to procure an abortion with a physic given to her by a shepherd, a physic with which, monstrously, the shepherd was accustomed to doctor his flock. The savagery of the conclusion lies in the fact that the daughter dies as her reluctant lover returns to make matrimonial amends.[30] The awakening passion and intimate secretiveness of young love is dampened in "The Conformers" by the sour anticipation of the staidness and monotony of marriage. Hardy can write charmingly and with a sympathetic warmth about young lovers, but he invariably taints the charm and the sympathy with the threat of marital dullness:

> Yes; we'll wed, my little fay,
> And you shall write you mine,
> And in a villa chastely gray
> We'll house, and sleep, and dine.
> But those night-screened, divine,

> Stolen trysts of heretofore,
> We of choice ecstasies and fine
> Shall know no more.[31]

Throughout the four stanzas the exaltation of the fresh excitement of pre-marital romance is put insistently in the negative: the contrasting damnation of the pedestrian nature of marriage is positive. The young lovers shall "*no more evade*" the betraying sunshine which reveals their clandestine love; they shall "*not* go in stealth" to unknown rendezvous; there will be "*no* leapings each to each." There is a certain malice in attitude in this premature blighting of young happiness which goes beyond the limit of possible compassionate antidote. Or is this some of Young's "gnarled and wintry phrasing"? Is this the bitter song of a man whose early, effulgent passion led to no marital peace? Was his wedding followed by:

> But syllables in a frigid tone
> Of household speech.[31]

It is difficult to determine how much stems from Hardy's own domestic unease, but there is a gibing clever shallowness about the last four lines which show the poet at his bleakest. When the lovers are dead people will not talk of their wild romance:

> But as they graveward glance
> Remark: "In them we lose
> A worthy pair, who helped advance
> Sound parish views."[31]

Against this caustic attitude to conventional marriage, we must set the strangely animated and emotionally paradoxical *Poems of 1912–13*, subtitled *Veteris vestigia flammae*. In the first chapter, I have tried to indicate something of the mystery clouding Hardy's domestic life, but have reached no determinate conclusion. Perhaps too much is being made over what was simply an unhappy

marriage. Certainly G. M. Young makes it uncompli-
cated of explanation, but from his first premise, he develops an adroit argument. He writes of Hardy's courtship at St Juliot:

> And what happened there was what has happened and
> will happen from one generation to another. He fell in
> love with a girl with whom he was not intellectually in
> key. There was no open catastrophe: only the fire sank
> rapidly into vacancy and chill. But by some mysterious
> power Hardy was able to preserve, encysted as it were,
> this early passion in all its primal intensity; and so it
> came about that some of the most poignant love-poems
> in our language were written by an old man out of his
> memories of forty years before.[32]

This is persuasively phrased and the argument of re-
invoking, after a span of forty years, an early romantic
magic is almost wholly true. The late-flowering inspiration is evident in "I Found her out there," "The Voice,"
"A Dream or No" among others. It is particularly dis-
cernible in a poem which, with geronthic pathos, Hardy
crystallises some of the inconsequential ramblings, the
gropings for her Plymouth girlhood, in Emma's *Recollections*:[33]

> Nobody thinks: There, there she lay
> In a room by the Hoe, like the bud of a flower.
> And listened, just after the bedtime hour,
> To the stammering chimes that used to play
> The quaint Old Hundred-and-Thirteenth tune
>     In Saint Andrew's tower
>     Night, morn, and noon.[34]

There are, nevertheless, certain poems in this group which
refer to phases of happiness in middle and late marriage,
long after the first fine ecstasy. The lines:

> Never to bid good-bye,
> Or lip me the softest call[35]

with their mock remonstrative affection, refer to Emma of old age: the anguished lostness of "Your Last Drive" and "The Walk" is in mourning for the later days of her life. The period of mid-marriage is cherished in "Without Ceremony" and "Lament"; and a fashion magazine which had arrived after Emma's death, recalls, with an elegiac matter-of-factness, in the poem "A Circular," the days when she was Hardy's "lady proud." It is almost certain that the personal mystery cannot be entirely resolved. There is no facile interpretation of Hardy's sexual attitudes either in prose or verse: if anything, *Poems of 1912–13* push valid explanation further away.

With *Satires of Circumstance* we return to the puckish mocking atmosphere of *Time's Laughingstocks*, but this time they are cynical jokes in miniature: a moment in the monotony of everyday is captured, arrested: then a word or a wink or a nod reveals the situation in its bitter drollness. In "At Tea" the young anonymous triangle sit apparently cosily and placidly: unexpectedly the dull homely scene becomes potent and alive with intrigue. The woman visitor is an old flame of the husband. But the moment of crisis flickers as surreptitiously as it does fleetingly. They relapse into pedestrian quasi-normalcy and:

> The guest sits smiling and sips her tea,
> And he throws her a stray glance yearningly.[36]

The satirical circumstances are "in fifteen glimpses" and the title of each invariably names the situation of the focalised incident—"In Church," "At a Watering Place," "In the Room of the Bride-elect." In an unguarded moment, in "Outside the Window," a girl has a shrill quarrel with her mother: this is innocently witnessed by her lover and she loses him.[37] "By her Aunt's Grave" recalls Solomon Longway's "Why *should* death rob life o' fourpence?" There is peasant realism rather than greed in the attitude of the young lover who suggests to his girl friend that they should spend her aunt's money on dance and revelry at the Load of Hay rather than on a headstone for her grave.[38] A further parallel with a prose fiction theme can be seen in "In the Nuptial Chamber." For Hardy, music was not only a pleasurable experience in itself, but it could have a grotesque, bewitching effect: it could condition neuroti- cally the behaviour of a sensitive listener. It has already been noticed how Car'line Aspent in "The Fiddler of the Reels" could unwittingly be in musical thrall to Mop Ollamoor. The lives of the young couple of "In the Nuptial Chamber" are momentarily isolated and a similar para-psychological bondage to a "mastering tune" is paraded in gnomish irony. The new bride leaps out of bed at the sound of "the town folk's cheery compliment" to their marriage and the metal of their marriage is immediately tarnished with suspicion:

> "O but you don't know! 'Tis the passionate air
> To which my old Love waltzed with me,
> And I swore as we spun that none should share
> My home, my kisses, till death, save he!
> And he dominates me and thrills me through,
> And it's he I embrace while embracing you!"[39]

Commonplace occasions conceal human sordidness in birth and death. The guilty wife in "In the Restaurant" can stretch betrayal no further: she has a tattered respect for her husband and feels that she can no longer "nightly take him into my arms." She pleads with her lover to elope and "bear the shame" of their unborn child, but our uncertainty of worldly caprice is reflected in our ignorance of their final decision.[39] "At the Draper's" shows another, a morbid faithlessness, when a doomed consumptive husband catches his wife ordering fashion- able mourning clothes.[39]

Though the themes of twisted love, faithlessness, death, peasant cunning, peasant exploited innocence, recur with a frequency which surprisingly does not stale, there are, here and there, direct statements of unqualified happiness. As if to substantiate his refutation of pessimism made in the *Apology* to *Late Lyrics and Earlier* (1922), Hardy begins the volume with a song simple in concept, unwintry, and revealing an unpolluted enjoyment of serene days:

> This is the weather the cuckoo likes,
>     And so do I;
> When showers betumble the chestnut spikes,
>     And nestlings fly:
> And the little brown nightingale bills his best,
> And they sit outside at "The Travellers' Rest,"
> And maids come forth sprig-muslin drest,
> And citizens dream of the south and west,
>     And so do I.[40]

Hardy's defence in the *Apology*, however, is not really of such innocent pieces as this. He wishes to refute charges against the darker poems:

And what is to-day, in allusions to the present author's pages, alleged to be "pessimism" is, in truth, only such "questionings" in the exploration of reality, and is the first step towards the soul's betterment, and the body's also.

The "questionings" are Wordsworth's "obstinate" ones. Hardy continues:

If I may be forgiven for quoting my own old words, let me repeat what I printed in this relation more than twenty years ago, and wrote much earlier, in a poem entitled "In Tenebris":

> *If way to the Better there be, it exacts a full*
>     *look at the Worst:*

that is to say, by the exploration of reality, and its frank recognition stage by stage along the survey, with an eye to the best consummation possible: briefly, evolutionary meliorism.[41]

The magazine-editors might certainly have argued that there is an element of casuistry in this apology, and it is certainly true that an author, at the mercy of his fired imagination, can lose control of his declared intention: and perhaps genuinely not realise that the control has gone. In any event it must be accepted that Hardy wrote down his approximate philosophy in good faith. It would seem that it is the label "pessimism" that he objects to as though it were a symptom of ethical leprosy. If we exclude this taboo word, then, it must nevertheless be admitted that in the poems, as in the fictive prose, the gloom is at times thick, inimically tangible. In the process of "exploration of reality" and of stepping towards "the soul's betterment," Hardy bent his art towards the dark underside of things. But does this Stygian mordancy really matter in today's uncertainty? What is the final effect of it on the sensitivity of a modern reader? Does it involve a transference of unoptimism which pushes us further towards suicidal despair?

I think not: there is always F. R. Leavis's massive devaluation which cannot be frivolously discounted: but it is difficult to make generalisations on a thousand poems. However, these dirges of peasant deceit, this twilight singing of violence and betrayal and tawdry death, of the fundamental unhappinesses, of metaphysical attitudes which arouse sombre meditation, have for some of us a haunting quality. They are frostily stimulating rather than morbidly depressing. When we surrender ourselves to their fields of poetic force, we are in grim, unfamiliar country; a country phenomenally tribed; a place which contains spectres and spiritual hoodlums; a place of malicious coincident and angrily turned accident. But there is also an agonising beauty, and in the prevailing weirdness there can be detected connexions with reality as we think we know it; there are flashes of terribly wise perception which make us uneasily aware that we are touching the roots of understanding. Fleeting brightnesses, too. Faces are turned sharply and furtively towards hopefulness; there are yearnings, not always stonily denied, for normalcy and moral sunniness; above all there is to be found compassion and pity for humankind under the weight of the weary world. But generally life is rewardless. The "evolutionary meliorism" is hard to trace. If there is any compensation, it lies only in the integrity of the suffering: the ultimate human supremacy over the sordid, even though humanity usually succumbs.

## REFERENCES

1. Douglas Brown, in his *Thomas Hardy*, entitles an excellent chapter "The Harvest of the Novels" and acknowledges his debt for the phrase to Ezra Pound.
2. V. H. Collins, *op. cit.*, p. 72.
3. *D., Preface*, p. x.
4. *D., Preface*, p. vii.
5. *D., Preface*, p. ix.
6. *D., Preface*, p. viii.
7. *D., Preface*, p. ix.
8. *D.*, Part First, Fore Scene.
9. *D.*, Part Third, After Scene.
10. J. O. Bailey, *Thomas Hardy and the Cosmic Mind*, 1956.
11. *D.*, Part Third, After Scene.
12. J. O. Bailey, *op. cit.*, pp. 173–4.
13. *D.*, Part Third, Act II. Sc. ii.
14. R. A. Scott-James, *op. cit.*, p. 35.
15. *Selected Poems of Thomas Hardy*, ed. G. M. Young, p. x.
16. F. R. Leavis, *New Bearings in English Poetry*, 1954, p. 59.
17. *C.P.*, p. 3.
18. *C.P.*, p. 9.
19. *C.P.*, p. 19.
20. *C.P.*, p. 26.
21. *C.P.*, p. 45.
22. *C.P.*, p. 78.
23. *C.P.*, p. 79.
24. *C.P.*, p. 80.
25. *C.P.*, p. 82.
26. *C.P.*, p. 127.
27. *C.P.*, p. 135.
28. *C.P.*, pp. 180–1.
29. *C.P.*, p. 185.
30. *C.P.*, p. 188.
31. *C.P.*, pp. 213–4. (my italics).
32. G. M. Young, *op. cit.*, p. xvi.

33. Evelyn Hardy and Robert Gittings, *op. cit.*, p. 12 and p. 70.
34. *C.P.*, p. 332.
35. *C.P.*, p. 318.
36. *C.P.*, p. 391.
37. *C.P.*, p. 394.
38. *C.P.*, p. 392.
39. *C.P.*, p. 396.
40. *C.P.*, p. 533.
41. *C.P.*, p. 526.

# CHAPTER VII

# ARTILLERY OF WORDS

Bacon quotes Sir Henry Wotton as saying, with a brutal sense of perspective, "that critics are like the brushers of noblemen's clothes." The interpretation of Anatole France is more idealistically diffuse: "Le bon critique est celui qui raconte les aventures de son âme au milieu des chefs-d'oeuvres." Critics of all breeds, clothes-brushers and soul-explorers, have lined up before the Hardyan literary catafalque. Comparable with his own creative energy, remarkably sustained over sixty years, is the amount of critical energy Hardy has provoked in others. It is a crowning posthumous irony that this writer, who was so patronisingly received by the earlier reviewers, should become the centre of so much highminded debate, so much intellectual marching and counter-marching, so often misinterpreted, so often definitively resolved. He is a peg on which diverse hats of literary fashion have been hung. In almost a century of critical writing the fashions have been as capricious as most. It is a long haul from the censorious sarcasm of the reviewer in the *Spectator* of 22 Apr. 1871, who was angered by the immorality in *Desperate Remedies*—

This is an absolutely anonymous story, no assumption of a nom-de-plume which might, at some future time, disgrace the family name, and still more the Christian name, of a repentant and remorseful novelist—and very right too. By all means let him bury the secret in the profoundest depths of his own heart, out of reach, if possible, of his own consciousness. The law is hardly just which prevents Tinsley Brothers from concealing their participation also[1]

—to A. J. Guerard's armoury of psycho-analysis, psychic sensitivity, and general critical sprightliness:

> We are in fact attracted by much that made the post-Victorian realist uneasy: the inventiveness and improbability, the symbolic use of reappearance and coincidence, the wanderings of a macabre imagination, the suggestions of supernatural agency; the frank acknowledgement that love is basically sexual and marriage usually unhappy; the demons of plot, irony and myth. And we are repelled or left indifferent by what charmed that earlier generation: the regionalist's ear for dialect, the botanist's eye for the minutiae of field and tree, the architect's eye for ancient mansions, and the farmer's eye for sheepshearings; the pretentious meditation on Egdon Heath; the discernible architecture of the novels and the paraphrasable metaphysic; the Franciscan tenderness and sympathy —and, I'm afraid, the finally unqualified faith in the goodness of a humanity more sinned against than sinning.[2]

I quote at length because this is an important declaration in an important book. There has been a complete critical *volte-face*: the reviewing fashion has radically altered from the attitude of the "post-Victorian Realists," from the attitude of such critics (although they had indeed perceptive ability worthy of the utmost respect) as Lionel Johnson, Lascelles Abercrombie, Samuel Chew, and H. C. Duffin. Such a critical reversal is a reaction to assessments of Hardy, *as a whole*: it may be the result of maturation or caprice—the cause of the reappraisal is dependent upon one's point of view. But there is also a school of thought which bisects Hardy as an artist: there can be no cohering valuation: he must be either a

novelist or a poet, and if he is one, the other is largely
ignored. F. R. Leavis and some of his disciples are at the
poetic pole in this matter. In H. Coombes' chapter in the
*Pelican Guide to English Literature*, Hardy is recognised as a
poet in stature somewhere between Walter de la Mare
and Edward Thomas. Hardy may well have been puzzled
by his position in the league, but he would have been
enormously pleased at being dubbed poet: perhaps even
with stoic forbearance of Coombes's Leavisite echo: "the
*small number* of his wonderful best poems."[3] However unfashionable it may be, I am convinced that it is immensely
rewarding to avoid catch-penny dichotomy, to look at *all*
Hardy's works and to recognise in them valuable inter-
relationship.

A. J. Guerard has been quoted already in this chapter
and in preceding ones, and the frequency of quotation is
a mark of readily-granted esteem and debt. Guerard,
from first to last, stresses the power of "the popular story-
telling of a singularly uninhibited imagination,"[4] but
although this is quite a dominant theme, the work is
thick with other distillations of an outstanding scholarly
and penetrative mind. There are occasional shrewd
references to the poetry, but the book's main concern, as
the title indicates, is with the novels and stories. The
latter-day conventional neglect of the stories and the
"minor" novels is rectified. The analysis of the better-
known heroes and heroines—especially the heroines—
surprises with its sharp excellences of reappraisal in mid-
twentieth-century terms, although "The Genealogy of
Hardy's Younger Women,"[5] despite its ingenuity and its
revelation of arguable character kinship, may be considered a shade facile and contrived. Admittedly all
Hardy's heroines have something in common, but
Guerard's baton-passing of hereditary characteristics is,
to my mind, overemphasised. This objection is small, as
is the one to his occasional predilection for technical
jargon. Not all readers would be immediately apprecia-

tive of the explanatory note he gives on "intuitive understanding":

> I use "intuitive understanding" in the sense given to it
> by psychologists when they speak of literary charac-
> terization. It refers to no less than all findings, conscious
> or subconscious, not based on formal experiment and
> analysis.[6]

These are but minor quibbles. *Thomas Hardy: The Novels
and Stories* is written by a man for whom Hardy obviously
means very much but who is not afraid to dispel old
shibboleths nor to point out limitations. It is highly intellectual without ever leaving the ground of common
humanity; it is written in compulsive lively prose with
wide and knowledgeable reference and allusion.

The standard work of reference is indubitably *The Life
of Thomas Hardy*, in two volumes, by Florence Emily
Hardy. It is fairly well accepted nowadays that there was
a deliberate act of camouflage in giving Florence Emily
the credit of authorship, and that the book, apart from
the last chapter or so of the second volume, was written
by Hardy himself. This is why, despite the book's immense value as a source of information, it must be handled
warily. Hardy only let the world know about himself (and
surely this is not culpable) what he wanted the world to
know. The absence of some facts can lead to a possible
distortion of submitted facts. Parts of the image are miss-
ing or unclear and therefore the presented image can be
misleading. An author, writing his own semi-critical
autobiography, is, as it were, picking himself up psychologically and artistically by his own boot-straps. After
this caution, however, the book is basically essential to
any student of Hardy's works, and it is imbued throughout
with the author's charming modesty and reticence. The
Prefatory Note begins:

> Mr. Hardy's feeling for a long time was that he would

not care to have his life written at all. And though often asked to record his recollections he would say that he "had not sufficient admiration for himself" to do so. But later, having observed many erroneous and grotesque statements advanced as his experiences, and a so-called "Life" published as authoritative, his hand was forced, and he agreed to my strong request that the facts of his career should be set down for use in the event of its proving necessary to print them.[7]

This is not mock-modesty or sham, even if Hardy himself dictated it.

Two critical works were published in 1954, by Evelyn Hardy and by Douglas Brown. Evelyn Hardy's *Thomas Hardy: A Critical Biography* is a scholarly work in that it is assiduously put together and most of the sources, both textual and critical, have been ransacked. Among its merits, it contains an excellent and ably-supported reconstruction of *The Poor Man and the Lady* which holds all the excitement of speculation on a deliberately destroyed manuscript. It is tantalising and frustrating that this fictive piece of juvenilia with its story of Will Strong and Miss Allamount, with its meetings of radicals in Trafalgar Square and an unexpected "kept mistress of an architect," is no longer extant. Evelyn Hardy has also edited *Thomas Hardy's Notebooks* (1955). These supplement to some extent Florence Emily's *Life* but they are largely concerned with interesting trivia. The letters from Julia Augusta Martin, Hardy's "lady of the manor," with the sadness of depleted fortune, carry a poignant charm and no more.

In Douglas Brown's *Thomas Hardy* a thesis is mounted. Brown's main theme is "the agricultural tragedy of 1870–1902" and the clash between the agricultural and urban modes of life. Yet this *motif*, persuasively and validly sustained, is not so much of a preoccupation as to disallow of sharp and powerful commentary on many aspects of Hardy's writing. Brown largely concentrates his critical energy on seven "major" novels and on certain shrewdly selected poems. He is not concerned with a dimidiation of the artist. Although he sees Hardy primarily as a poet, he writes cogently and warmly of the "novels of character and environment." Although quoting Ezra Pound on the *Collected Poems*:

> Now *there* is clarity. There *is* the harvest of having written 20 novels first.[8]

and although he takes his chapter title on the poetry from the quotation, he is no denigrator of the prose fiction. He comments on the prose period:

> True, he was a poet first, and continued practising his poetry throughout those years; and when he was able, in the later years, to devote all his energies to the poet's vocation, he achieved in poetry a distinction as unique as any he achieved in fiction. But we should not be misled by his occasional and bitter derogation of his achievement as a novelist.[9]

Nor, it may be added, should we be misled by a recent fashionable cult with similar derogative tendencies. Brown, it would seem, sees the fictive prose writing—or at least what he judges to be the superior section of it— as being both triumphant artistic completenesses *and* as a necessary salutary apprenticeship in the progression of a poet: the experience of the fiction writer nurtured the latent versifier. As Brown puts it, "There, in one style of art, he discovered those situations of the spirit he could best identify and celebrate in verse."[9]

There are inevitably vast gulfs of critical attitude and demeanour between Douglas Brown and H. C. Duffin, whose *Thomas Hardy: A Study of the Wessex Novels* was published in 1916. When the present-day reader comes to Chapter IIA, "Hardy's Women: Hardy's View of Woman," the very title informs him that there will be opportunity for an intellectual snigger; but if we are de-

terred by an overlay of archaic chivalry and of a social
approach to woman—"woman *ipsa*"—as obsolete as her
hobble skirt, then we shall indubitably miss a genuine
and warm essay at "advanced" sexual thinking; we shall
fail to recognise the varying impacts that Hardy made on
successive generations. When we read on Sue Bridehead:
"she is capable of estimating right and wrong by argument; she could have met Clare and Henry Knight on
their own ground. She is less the woman for it: argument
is man's prerogative (or penalty)";[10] when we learn that
Troy is one "whom any man knows to be a dirty scoundrel
the moment he sets eyes on him";[11] and when we
consider Bathsheba's "sex's cardinal fault—jealousy" and
its decisive importance in her relations with the sergeant:

> Nine women out of ten would be attracted by Troy:
> eight out of ten would prefer him to Oak and Bold-
> wood; and seven out of ten (this is a business-like and
> cautious age, or the ratio would be greater) would let
> jealousy overrule their judgement as Bathsheba Ever-
> dene did[11]

—we must at these moments allow for the handicap of the
extra weight of scepticism we have had to carry since
1916. Despite this embarrassing penchant for a dated
propriety, despite a certain cloudiness in character-
analysis, there is an infectious enthusiasm about Duffin's
writing, and, underneath it all, an unexpected perception,
much of which is valid today. Above all, Duffin is a critic
unbloated by self-importance; he is aware of the para-
sitical nature of his craft; he is humble with the knowledge that his own imaginative criticism is nurtured by
the creative imagination of the writers and he makes his
judgments therefore with appropriate diffidence. Such
literary seemliness, on Duffin's part, far outweighs his
Edwardian attitudes.

Lionel Johnson is another, courteous writer, guided by
self-knowledge and truly cognisant of his own and his

H

age's limitations. In his Preface to *The Art of Thomas Hardy* (1894) the note of scholarly humility is at once struck:

> It is held, upon all hands, that to write about the works of a living writer is a difficult and delicate thing: I have felt the inevitable difficulty; I have tried to preserve the becoming delicacy. Throughout these essays upon the works of Mr. Hardy, there will be found, I trust, no discourtesy in my censure: I trust still more, no impertinence in my praise.[12]

It is important to remember that this was written before *Jude* and *The Dynasts* and before the publication of the volumes of poetry, and that Johnson is limited to a consideration of Hardy's "fifteen published works." There are obvious disadvantages in standing too close to the picture. One may see detail with insistent and demanding clarity, whereas, moving away, and in balanced perspective, these items would be merged and muted. A certain distortion is apparent in Johnson's avuncular appraisal of the insipid Faith Julian: "Perhaps none of these strong and quiet women is more gently attractive, than Faith Julian; whom one does not immediately learn to esteem at her true value: it requires the wearying agility of Ethelberta's ambition, to set off the restful charm of Faith."[13] There is, too, an overpraising of the men characters, compared with the women, which is in inverse proportion to A. J. Guerard's assessment; but this could equally be the result of moral conditioning as of peering too minutely at the canvas. Perhaps, what would strike us today as one of the most myopic judgments, lies in the tempering of Hardy to the sensitive lamb, by implying, through Hardy's knowledge of ecclesiastics, a vague support for the Church:

> Mr. Hardy's divines must not be left without a word of gratitude: they are of many kinds, and all excellent.

There is old Mr. Clare, the most lovable of stern Cal-
vinists: the Baptist minister, whom young Somerset
confronted upon Paedobaptism, for the support of the
backsliding Paula: the Bishop of Melchester, so cruelly
fooled in his marriage: Mr. Swancourt, a genial
aristocrat with the gout, beneficed at the ends of the
earth: others, whose acquaintance we make best
through the criticisms of their flocks.[14]

Perhaps it is inevitable that immediately preceding
generations are faintly ludicrous in their necessarily
square pronouncements. One mark of greatness is survival, despite the derision of unstable fashions, which
always, at their moment of dominance, appeal through
their up-to-date knowingness. To despise or ignore critics
like Duffin or Johnson because they breathed the moral
air of 1894 or of 1916 is to forgo a rewarding critical experience. Hardy's transcendance of such yellowing
morality makes him all the more remarkable.

On 9 Apr. 1920, V. H. Collins practically forced his
way into Max Gate. The reason for such behaviour on the
part of one obviously so fastidious and so correct is largely
given in the Introduction to *Talks with Thomas Hardy*
(1928): Hardy's poems had "a supreme significance" for
him and "for many years I had felt as Browning felt about
Byron when he said that he would 'at any time have gone
to see a curl of his hair or one of his gloves'."[15] It would
seem that the octogenarian author was not unpleased by
the intrusion, perhaps because here was an uninhibited
enthusiast for the poems; and the book is the record of a
series of tea-time intimacies, set out in dramatic form.
Collins, however, apparently botched the first publication of the book and it contains a number of mistakes—a
fact which annoyed Florence Emily. The conversations
are, of course, for the Hardy student, fascinating, but it is
strange that for all his professed enthusiasm, Collins
shows a remarkable lack of appreciation of some of the

poetry. Hardy's answers to a series of questions, put to him by Collins who was asking for elucidation, are unsurprisingly laconic. One of the few replies which is not monosyllabic is: "I think you will be able to work it out."[16] Almost all the questions are quite incredibly naïve. Whilst retaining salutarily in mind Hardy's age, which may not unnaturally cloud fact with a certain wistful reminiscence, these faithfully-set-down minutiae of a few hours of the twilight years shed a wintry illumination. It was not, it seems, only the press attacks on *Jude* which caused Hardy to give up such art: "I never cared very much about writing novels."[17] There is passing comment on Johnson, Abercrombie, "Professor Chew," "Mr. Hedgcock," and "the professor from Tokio," who explained why only the first half of *Tess* had been translated into Japanese: "the latter portion of the book would not appeal to the Japanese. It would be outside their comprehension. In Japan it is thought a virtuous thing for a girl to sell herself to obtain money for the help of her family. There would not seem to them to be any tragedy in Tess living with Alec d'Urberville."[18] There is, also, unimportant chat about current prices of second editions of Hardy's work alongside of reported evidence of the pains he took over accuracy of detail. Commenting on the juridical advice he took from experts to establish legal verisimilitude in the story "On The Western Circuit," he reveals an old man's delight in pedagogic contradiction.[19] And there is much to delight, if mainly of a lightweight nature, in V. H. Collins's enthusiastic records.

The flow of critical commentary, as my bibliography indicates, continues up to the moment of writing, and one can see no sign of abatement. I am not concerned with the denigration in some quarters of the prose fiction: such a fashion is as about as stable as Paula's pink flannel gymnasium costume. There have been, however, two intriguing books published recently and one earnestly wishes that their findings could be accepted without hedging. Students of Hardy's writings are perplexed by the enigmatic bias in most of his work: there is the familiar sludge of bitterness, the tenaciously-held pessimism at the bottom of all the brightnesses, the laughter, the exuberance, the compassion: it seems to hold the author in thrall, so much so that he equivocally, sometimes querulously, denies it. These two books—J. O. Bailey's *Thomas Hardy and the Cosmic Mind* and a combined work on Emma's *Some Recollections* by Evelyn Hardy and Robert Gittings—attempt to explain away something of the prejudice. For me the attempts are not wholly successful, but each, in their very different ways, make a persuasive and fascinating argument.

Bailey's erudite book, already cited, shows its author elaborately enthusiastic about evolutionary meliorism:

> Hardy's meaning, I think, is that when men develop compassion and strive to establish a kindlier race in a better world, their desire may influence the Mind as, say, prayer is presumed to influence God, and the Mind, operating through impulses upon life-processes that are slightly variable in the areas of generation— upon mutations—will offer the aid It is free to offer.[20]

Bailey quotes Hardy's substantiation of such an outlook in William Archer's *Real Conversations*: and Hardy's sincerity is not questioned: he reiterates the theme, as I have already shown, in the *Apology* of 1922. But in his creative work the meliorism seems to be a long time in *evolving*: the prospective betterment is on so distant a horizon that the people in his novels and poems, and perhaps the readers of them, have little to turn to spiritually apart from orthodox doctrines: for those for whom Church consolation is insufficient, evolutionary meliorism is not much better: in fact it is not mentioned as such, and is only present by devious implication. The immediate realities must be acknowledged: in terms of general philosophy, Hardy's fictive world is sick: in terms of the particular, the badness is centred on sexual relationships and marriage.

It is this latter aspect which is the concern of Evelyn Hardy and Gittings, and a certain exoneration of Emma and contrition of Thomas is propounded. Emma's pathetic doodling, sometimes fired by a delirious imagination, occupies two-thirds of the book, but one must sometimes agree with Evelyn Hardy: "Feeling carries her forward where craftsmanship and artistry are lacking, and Emma Hardy's pages give off something of that live quality which attracted Hardy, both as a writer and a man."[21] But whatever the interests, it is senile doodling at the dying end of a life which held we know not what of misery, delusion, and domestic disharmony. Hardy has meticulously corrected the untidy manuscript, and the editors see in his close reading of it, apart from a possible intention to publish it, a biting self-recrimination and remorse on his part as though the fault of the unhappy marriage were largely his. This is indeed possible, but, since nobody really knows, I suggest unlikely. In *Some Recollections* Emma reveals herself as an artless, rather stupid and limited girl from a Plymouth family which later lived near the bone of penurious respectability. She was no longer in the flush of maidenhood, had suffered some premonitory illnesses and had moved to St Juliot when she met Hardy: there a romantic figure, scampering across the hills on a pony (the parallel with Elfride is too obvious), she captured his heart. We must always bear in mind the unknown barriers through which the aging Emma had dragged these recollections. One, or a series of them, as Gittings points out, is revealed in "The Interloper."[22] "The visage of Madness" appears to have been a cruel, insistent threat. There is indubitably an alliance between *Some Recollections* and certain poems which the editors of this book justly claim. Perhaps the frankest statement is contained in a stanza in "After A Journey":

Yes: I have re-entered your olden haunts at last;
   Through the years, through the dead scenes I have
      tracked you;
What have you now found to say of our past—
   Scanned across the dark space wherein I have lacked
      you?
Summer gave us sweets, but autumn wrought division?
   Things were not lastly as firstly well
         With us twain, you tell?
But all's closed now, despite Time's derision.[23]

But even this statement is qualified by question marks.
There is basically no exoneration, no explanation. The
causative factors for the sexual unhappinesses, for a "full
look at the Worst," are as hard to trace as the evolutionary meliorism.

One wonders whether, in the long run, this really
matters. In Hardy's writings a "full look at the Worst"
involves a hard, continual staring at it. Despite large
areas of fun and exuberance, there are obsessional tendencies towards an increasing entanglement in inimical
undergrowth: and the processes of cutting through it, to
discover "a way to the better" are arduous, seemingly
impossible. Given prevalent conditions over the last
hundred years, given our paradoxical state of human
development, that could be Hardy's fundamental truth.

## REFERENCES

1. *F.E.H.(I).*, p. 110.
2. *A.J.G.*, p. 6.
3. H. Coombes, in *The Pelican Guide to English Literature*, Vol. 7. 1961, p. 145. (my italics).
4. *A.J.G.*, p. 158.
5. *A.J.G.*, p. 141.
6. *A.J.G.*, p. 102.
7. *F.E.H.(I).*, p. vii.
8. Douglas Brown, *op. cit.*, p. 145.
9. Douglas Brown, *op. cit.*, pp. 146–7.
10. H. C. Duffin, *Thomas Hardy*, 1921, p. 136.

11. H. C. Duffin, *op. cit.*, p. 139.

12. Lionel Johnson, *op. cit.*, p. v.

13. Lionel Johnson, *op. cit.*, p. 215.

14. Lionel Johnson, *op. cit.*, p. 221.

15. V. H. Collins, *op. cit.*, p. ix.

16. V. H. Collins, *op. cit.*, p. 23.

17. V. H. Collins, *op. cit.*, p. 42.

18. V. H. Collins, *op. cit.*, p. 65.

19. V. H. Collins, *op. cit.*, p. 77.

20. J. O. Bailey, *op. cit.*, p. 179.

21. Evelyn Hardy and Robert Gittings, *op. cit.*, p. xiv.

22. Evelyn Hardy and Robert Gittings, *op. cit.*, p. 78 and *C.P.*, p. 458.

23. Evelyn Hardy and Robert Gittings, *op. cit.*, p. 86 and *C.P.*, p. 328.

# BIBLIOGRAPHY

*In all cases in which two or more editions of any work are cited, all references in the text are to the edition marked * in this Bibliography.*

## I. THOMAS HARDY

Fuller information may be found in R. L. Purdy, *Thomas Hardy, A Bibliographical Study*, 1954, to which the author is much indebted. The Wessex Edition, published in 24 vols. between 1912 and 1931, is universally regarded as definitive. M.L.E. = the Macmillan Library Edition.

### *1. Novels*

*The Poor Man and the Lady*. Written in 1868, but never published.

*Desperate Remedies*. London 1871. *M.L.E., London 1960. New York (St. Martin's Press).

*Under the Greenwood Tree, or the Mellstock Quire*. London 1872. *M.L.E., London 1960. New York (St. Martin's Press).

*A Pair of Blue Eyes*, in *Tinsleys' Magazine*, Sep. 1872–Jul. 1873. London 1873. *M.L.E., London 1957. New York (St. Martin's Press).

*Far from the Madding Crowd*, in *Cornhill Magazine*, Jan.–Dec. 1874. London 1874. *M.L.E., London 1958. New York (St. Martin's Press).

*The Hand of Ethelberta, A Comedy in Chapters*, in *Cornhill Magazine*, Jul. 1875–May 1876. London 1876. *M.L.E., London 1960. New York (St. Martin's Press).

*The Return of the Native*, in *Belgravia*, Jan.–Dec. 1878. London 1878. *M.L.E., London 1961. New York (St. Martin's Press).

*The Trumpet-Major*, in *Good Words*, Jan.–Dec. 1880. London 1880. *M.L.E., London, 1960. New York (St. Martin's Press).

*A Laodicean, A Story of Today*, in *Harper's New Monthly Magazine* (European edn), Dec. 1880–Dec. 1881. New York and London 1881. *M.L.E., London 1951. New York (St. Martin's Press).

*Two on a Tower*, in the *Atlantic Monthly* (Boston), May–Dec. 1882, and simultaneously in England. London 1882. *M.L.E., London 1960.

*The Mayor of Casterbridge, The Life and Death of a Man of Character*, in the *Graphic*, Jan.—May 1886. London 1886. *M.L.E., London 1958. New York (St. Martin's Press).

*The Woodlanders*, in *Macmillan's Magazine*, May 1886–Apr. 1887. London and New York 1887. *M.L.E., London 1958. New York (St. Martin's Press).

*Tess of the d'Urbervilles, A Pure Woman Faithfully Presented*, in the *Graphic*, Jul.–Dec. 1891. London 1891. \*M.L.E., London 1960. New York (St. Martin's Press).

*Jude the Obscure*, in *Harper's New Monthly Magazine*, Dec. 1894–Nov. 1895, simultaneously in New York and London. London 1896. \*M.L.E., London 1960. New York (St. Martin's Press).

*The Well-Beloved, A Sketch of a Temperament*, (entitled *The Pursuit of the Well-Beloved*) in the *Illustrated London News*, Oct.–Dec. 1892. London 1897. \*M.L.E., London 1960. New York (St. Martin's Press).

### 2. Stories

"Destiny and a Blue Cloak," in *The New York Times*, Oct. 1874. Uncollected.

"An Indiscretion in the life of an Heiress," in *New Quarterly Magazine*, Jul. 1878, and simultaneously in *Harper's Weekly*. London (privately printed) 1934.

*Wessex Tales*. London and New York 1888. \*M.L.E., London 1960. New York (St. Martin's Press). Originally contained: "The Distracted Preacher" (as "The Distracted Young Preacher," in *New Quarterly Magazine*, Apr. 1879); "Fellow-Townsmen" (in *New Quarterly Magazine*, Apr. 1880); "The Three Strangers" (in *Longman's Magazine*, Mar. 1883); "Interlopers at the Knap" (in the *English Illustrated Magazine*, May 1884); and "The Withered Arm" (in *Blackwood's Edinburgh Magazine*, Jan. 1888).

*A Group of Noble Dames*. London 1891. \*M.L.E., London 1952. New York (St. Martin's Press). Contained: "The Duchess of Hamptonshire" (as "The Impulsive Lady of Croome Castle," in *Light*, Apr. 1878); "The Honourable Laura" (as "Benighted Travellers," in the *Bolton Weekly Journal*, Dec. 1881); "The First Countess of Wessex" (in *Harper's New Monthly Magazine*, Dec. 1889); "The Lady Penelope" (in *Longman's Magazine*, Jan. 1890); and "Barbara of the House of Grebe," "The Marchioness of Stonehenge," "Lady Mottisfont," "Squire Petrick's Lady," "The Lady Icenway," and "Anna, Lady Baxby" (all in the *Graphic*, Christmas Number, 1890).

*Life's Little Ironies*. London 1894. \*M.L.E., London 1952. New York (St. Martin's Press). Originally contained: "A Tradition of Eighteen Hundred and Four" (as "A Legend of the Year Eighteen Hundred and Four," in *Harper's Christmas*, Dec. 1882; later transferred to *Wessex Tales*); "A Tragedy of Two Ambitious" (in *The Universal Review*, Dec. 1888); "The Melancholy Hussar of the German Legion" (as "The Melancholy Hussar," in the *Bristol Times and Mirror*, Jan. 1890; later transferred to *Wessex Tales*); "A Few Crusted Characters" (as "Wessex Folk," in *Harper's New*

*Monthly Magazine*, Mar.–Jun. 1891); "For Conscience' Sake," (in the *Fortnightly Review*, Mar. 1891); "To Please his Wife" (in *Black and White*, Jun. 1891); "On the Western Circuit" (in the *English Illustrated Magazine*, Dec. 1891); "The Son's Veto" (in the *Illustrated London News*, Christmas Number 1891); "The Fiddler of the Reels" (in *Scribner's Magazine*, May 1893); and "An Imaginative Woman" (in *Pall Mall Magazine*, Apr. 1894).

*A Changed Man and Other Tales*. London 1913. *M.L.E., London 1951 New York (St. Martin's Press). Contained: "What the Shepherd Saw" (in the *Illustrated London News*, Christmas Number 1881); "The Romantic Adventures of a Milkmaid" (in the *Graphic*, Summer Number 1883); "A Tryst at an Ancient Earthwork" (as "Ancient Earthworks and what two Enthusiastic Scientists Found therein," in the *Detroit Post*, Mar. 1885; and as "Ancient Earthworks at Casterbridge," in the *English Illustrated Magazine*, Dec. 1893); "A Mere Interlude" (in the *Bolton Weekly Journal*, Oct. 1885); "Alicia's Diary" (in the *Manchester Weekly Times*, Oct. 1887); "The Waiting Supper" (in *Murray's Magazine*, Jan. and Feb. 1888); "Master John Horsleigh, Knight" (in the *Illustrated London News*, Summer Number 1893); "A Committee-Man of 'The Terror' " (in the *Illustrated London News*, Christmas Number 1896); "The Duke's Reappearance" (in the *Saturday Review*, Christmas Supplement 1896); "The Grave by the Handpost" (in *St. James's Budget*, Christmas Number 1897); "A Changed Man" (in the *Sphere*, Apr. 1900); and "Enter a Dragoon" (in *Harper's Monthly Magazine*, Dec. 1900).

### 3. Verse

*Wessex Poems and Other Verses*. London 1898. New York (St. Martin's Press).

*Poems of the Past and Present*. London 1901.

*Time's Laughingstocks and Other Verses*. London 1909. New York (St. Martin's Press).

*Satires of Circumstance. Lyrics and Reveries*. London 1914.

*Moments of Vision and Miscellaneous Verses*. London 1917.

*Late Lyrics and Earlier with Many Other Verses*. London 1922.

*Human Shows, Far Fantasies, Songs and Trifles*. London 1925. New York (St. Martin's Press) 2 vols.

*Winter Words, in Various Moods and Metres*. London 1928.

*Collected Poems*. London 1930. *London 1960.

### 4. Drama

*The Dynasts. A Drama of the Napoleonic Wars:* Part First, London 1903–4; Part Second, London 1906; Part Third, London 1908. *Pocket edn., London 1958. New York (St. Martin's Press).

*The Famous Tragedy of the Queen of Cornwall at Tintagel in Lyonnesse.*
London 1923. Pocket edn., London 1958. New York (St.
Martin's Press).

### 5. Miscellaneous

"How I built myself a House," in *Chambers's Journal*, Mar. 1865.

"The Dorsetshire Labourer," in *Longman's Magazine*, Jul. 1883.

*The Dorset Farm Labourer, Past and Present.* Dorchester 1884.

"The Rev. William Barnes, B.D.," in the *Athenaeum*, Oct. 1886.

"Candour in English Fiction," in the *New Review*, VOL. II (1890),
No. 8.

*Selected Poems of William Barnes*, ed., with pref. and glossarial notes,
Thomas Hardy. London 1908.

Fuller details concerning uncollected letters, obituaries, speeches,
etc., may be found in Purdy, *Thomas Hardy, A Bibliographical Study*,
pp. 289–325.

### II. OTHERS

ABERCROMBIE, LASCELLES: *Thomas Hardy: A Critical Study*, first pub.
1912, *London 1919.

ARCHER, WILLIAM: *Real Conversations*, London 1904.

BAILEY, J. O.: "Hardy's Mephistophelean Visitants," in *PMLA*, LXI
(Dec. 1946), pp. 1146–84.

——: *Thomas Hardy and the Cosmic Mind*, North Carolina 1956.

BEACH, J. W.: *The Technique of Thomas Hardy*, Chicago 1922.

BLUNDEN, EDMUND: *Thomas Hardy*, London 1941. New York (St.
Martin's Press).

BOWRA, SIR M.: *The Lyrical Poetry of Thomas Hardy*, Byron Foundation
Lecture, Nottingham 1946.

BRAYBROOKE, PATRICK: *Thomas Hardy and his Philosophy*, Philadelphia
1927, London 1928.

BRENNECKE, ERNEST: *Thomas Hardy's Universe*, London 1924.

BROWN, DOUGLAS: *Thomas Hardy'* first pub. 1954; *rev. edn, London
1961. New York 1954.

CECIL, LORD DAVID: *Hardy the Novelist*, first pub. 1943; *London
1960.

CHAIKIN, MILTON: "A Possible Source of Hardy's *The Well-Beloved*,"
in *Modern Language Notes*, LXXI (1956), pp. 496–7.

CHAKRAVARTY, A. C.: *The Dynasts and the Post-war Age in Poetry*, London 1938.

CHAPMAN, F.: "Hardy the Novelist," in *Scrutiny*, III (Jun. 1934), pp.
22–37.

CHASE, M. E.: *Thomas Hardy from Serial to Novel*, Minneapolis 1927.

CHEW, SAMUEL C.: *Thomas Hardy, Poet and Novelist*, New York 1928.

CHILD, H.: *Thomas Hardy*, London 1916.

CHURCH, RICHARD: "Thomas Hardy as revealed in *The Dynasts*," in *Etudes Anglaises*, VII (1954), pp. 70–79.

CLIFFORD, EMMA: "The 'Trumpet-Major Notebook' and *The Dynasts*," in *Review of English Studies*, n.s., VIII (1957) pp. 149–161.

COLLINS, V. H.: *Talks with Thomas Hardy at Max Gate 1920–22*, London 1928.

COOMBES, H.: "Hardy, De La Mare and Edward Thomas," in *The Pelican Guide to English Literature*, VOL. VII, London 1961.

DAICHES, DAVID: *A Critical History of English Literature*, VOL. II, London 1960.

DAY, LEWIS, C.: *Lyrical Poetry of Thomas Hardy*, New York 1953.

DIKE, D. A.: "A Modern Oedipus: *The Mayor of Casterbridge*," in *Essays in Criticism*, II (1952), pp. 169–79.

DUFFIN, H. C.: *Thomas Hardy: A Study of the Wessex Novels*, first pub. 1916: *London 1921; rev. edn London 1937.

ELLIOTT, A. P.: *Fatalism in the Works of Thomas Hardy*, Philadelphia 1935.

ELLIS, HAVELOCK: "Thomas Hardy's Novels," in *Westminster Review*, n.s., LXIII (1883), pp. 334–64.

——: "Concerning *Jude the Obscure*," in *Savoy*, III (1896), pp. 35–49.

D'EXIDEUIL, PIERRE: *The Human Pair in the Works of Thomas Hardy*, tr. F. W. Crosse, London 1930.

FIROR, R. A.: *Folkways in Thomas Hardy*, Philadelphia 1931.

GARWOOD, HELEN: *Thomas Hardy: An Illustration of the Philosophy of Schopenhauer*, Philadelphia 1911.

GOLDBERG, M. A.: "Hardy's Double-Visioned Universe," in *Essays in Criticism*, VII (1957), pp. 374–82.

GOLDMAN, IRVING: "Evolution and Anthropology," in *Victorian Studies*, III (1959), pp. 55–75.

GOODHEART, EUGENE: "Thomas Hardy and the Lyrical Novel," in *Nineteenth Century Fiction*, XII (1957), pp. 215–225.

GRIMSDITCH, H. B.: *Character and Environment in the Novels of Thomas Hardy*, London 1925.

GUERARD, ALBERT J.: *Thomas Hardy: The Novels and Stories*, Cambridge, Mass., 1949.

HARDY, EVELYN: *Thomas Hardy: A Critical Biography*, London and New York 1954.

——: *Thomas Hardy's Notebooks*, London 1955. New York 1956.

—— and ROBERT GITTINGS (edd.): *Some Recollections by Emma Hardy together with Some Relevant Poems by Thomas Hardy*. London 1961.

HARDY, F. E.: *The Early Life of Thomas Hardy, 1840–91*, London 1928.

——: *The Later Years of Thomas Hardy, 1892–1928*, London 1930.

HARPER, C. G.: *The Hardy Country*, London 1904.

HAWKINS, DESMOND: *Thomas Hardy*, London 1950.

HEDGCOCK, F. A.: *Thomas Hardy: Penseur et Artiste*, Paris 1911.

HOLLAND, NORMAN: "*Jude the Obscure:* Hardy's Symbolic Indictment of Christianity," in *Nineteenth Century Fiction*, IX (1954), pp. 50–60.

HOLLOWAY, J.: *The Victorian Sage*, London 1953.

HOOPES, KATHLEEN R.,: "Illusion and Reality in *Jude the Obscure*," in *Nineteenth Century Fiction*, XII (1957), pp. 154–7.

HYDE, W. J.: "Hardy's View of Realism: A Key to the Rustic Characters," in *Victorian Studies*, II (1958), pp. 45–59.

HYNES, SAMUEL: *The Pattern of Hardy's Poetry*, Oxford 1961.

JOHNSON, LIONEL: *The Art of Thomas Hardy*, London 1895.

KETTLE, ARNOLD: *An Introduction to the English Novel*, VOL. II, first pub. 1953; \*London 1961.

KLINGOPULOS, G. D.: "Hardy's Tales Ancient and Modern," in *The Pelican Guide to English Literature*, VOL. VI, London 1958.

LAWRENCE, D. H.: "Study of Thomas Hardy," in *Phoenix: The Posthumous Papers of D. H. Lawrence*, ed. Edward C. MacDonald, New York 1950.

LEA, HERMANN: *Thomas Hardy's Wessex*, London 1913.

LEAVIS, F. R.: *New Bearings in English Poetry*, first pub. 1932; \*London 1954.

——: "Reality and Sincerity," in *Scrutiny*, 1952.

MACDONNELL, ANNIE: *Thomas Hardy*, London 1894.

MACDOWALL, A. S.: *Thomas Hardy: A Critical Study.* London 1931.

MEUSEL, MAGDALENE: *Thomas Hardy und die Bibel*, Kiel 1937.

MIZENER, ARTHUR: "*Jude the Obscure* as a Tragedy," in *Southern Review*, VI (1940).

MOYNAHAN, JULIAN: "*The Mayor of Casterbridge* and the Old Testament's First Book of Samuel: A Study of some Literary Relationships," in *PMLA*, LXXI (1956), pp. 118–30.

MUIR, EDWIN: "The Novels of Thomas Hardy," in *Essays on Literature and Society*, 1949.

NEVINSON, HENRY W.: *Thomas Hardy*, London 1941.

OLIPHANT, MRS M.: "The Anti-Marriage League," in *Blackwood's Magazine*, CLIX (1896), pp. 135–49.

PATERSON, J.: "*The Mayor of Casterbridge* as Tragedy," in *Victorian Studies*, III (1959), pp. 151–72.

PECKHAM, MORSE: "Darwinism and Darwinisticism," in *Victorian Studies*, III (1959), pp. 19–40.

PORTER, KATHARINE ANNE: "Notes on a Criticism of Thomas Hardy," in *The Southern Review*, VI (1940).

PURDY, RICHARD L.: *Thomas Hardy. A Bibliographical Study*, London, New York, Toronto 1954.

RICHARDS, I. A.: *Science and Poetry*, London 1926.

RUTLAND, W. R.: *Thomas Hardy: A Study of His Writings and Their Background*, Oxford 1938. New York 1962.

SAXELBY, F. O.: *Thomas Hardy Dictionary*, New York n.d.

cott-James, R. A.: *Thomas Hardy*, first pub. 1951; *London 1957.

*elected Poems of Thomas Hardy*, ed. G. M. Young, first pub. 1940; *London 1960.

hort, Clarice: "In Defense of Ethelberta," in *Nineteenth Century Fiction*, xiii (1958), pp. 48–57.

lack, Robert C.: "The Text of Hardy's *Jude the Obscure*," in *Nineteenth Century Fiction*, xi (1957), pp. 261–75.

outhworth, J. G.: *The Poetry of Thomas Hardy*, New York 1947.

pivey, Ted R.: "Thomas Hardy's Tragic Hero," in *Nineteenth Century Fiction*, ix (1954), pp. 179–191.

tewart, J. I. M.: "The Integrity of Hardy," in *English Studies*, i (1948), pp. 1–27.

ymons, A.: *A Study of Thomas Hardy*, London 1927.

veber, C. J.: *Hardy of Wessex. His Life and Literary Career*, New York 1940.

——: *Hardy in America*, Waterville, Maine, 1946.

——: *Hardy and the Lady from Madison Square*, Waterville, Maine, 1952.

vebster, H. C.: *On a Darkling Plain: The Art and Thought of Thomas Hardy*, Chicago 1947.

williams, R.: *The Wessex Novels*, London 1924.

windle, Bertram C. A.: *The Wessex of Thomas Hardy*, London 1902.

wing, George: "Tess and the Romantic Milkmaid," in *Review of English Literature*, iii (1962), pp. 22–30.